"Be surprised when your dog does something wrong, not right"

Kevin Pattison

King West Press

Published by King West Press 2009

www.kingwestpress.com

Dedication

This book is dedicated to Dezdamona (Dez), a Boarder Collie-Australian Heeler cross and her brother Maxamillion (Max) my super-smart Boarder Collie.

Their example has helped me to see how canine-to-canine and canine-to-human communication really works. From their play, protection, and interactions with others, my amazing dogs have made me realize just how little we understand about the animals we live with on a daily basis and that we require so much from.

Dez and Max are examples of dogs at their very best. Their generosity and wisdom have humbled me many times. They have touched my life and inspired my work, in ways that continue  to amaze me, even to this day.

A testament to the bond that can be shared between man and dog, I treasure all the days they walked beside me as true and loyal friends. Without their inspiration, this book would not exist.

Acknowledgments

First, I must thank all of the clients who believed in me and trusted in my training techniques.

Secondly, to all of the dogs that put up with their owners' learning struggles: they proved that they were smarter than they were given credit for. I especially, appreciate the many dogs that taught me how fast they could really move their mouths!

Thanks also to all of the condescending, negative, and unkind people who could not see that the world needs new teaching methods. It is their lazy satisfaction that drives me to reach above and beyond the current status quo. I cherish all of the people who thought that I was wrong, stupid or who simply believed my methods wouldn't work. I especially thank three ladies I met at a dog show in 1989, who were adamant that dogs can't learn beyond the training-level required to meet "show" purposes.

I am not being facetious. I truly appreciate what they said.

The doubt they expressed that day gave me just the motivation and incentive I needed, and helped me find my calling: to help show the world what is truly possible in dog training.

My heartfelt thanks go to Rich Pollack (aka: Richie), Mark Bewer, Rob and Bear Bowman, James Beebe, Brent Ross, Nancy Wright, Gio ("elb"), Kerry Cooper, and Brent and Tony Dobson. All of you have expanded my knowledge through brainstorming sessions and sharing your points of view. A sincere thanks to Peggy Stirrett and Stephen Shepherdson for their motivating words, constructive criticism, and the many memories we have of training Rocky and bailing Kyra out of "jail". To Stephanie, Jan, Dani, Joey, and Michael Gryckiewicz, I thank you for putting up with my crazy antics and for allowing me to use your kids for both the photo shoots and video footage. Not to forget Sydney, the old wise one, and Murphy, the latest addition to your family.

A gracious "thank you" to Todd Keating for all of the technical support, and for inputting all of the illustrations and photos during the production of this book.

A special thanks to my father, Ken Pattison, and my brothers, Kevin and Kurt, who reinforced at an early age that to win, one sometimes needs to first endure losing. They taught me to always look beyond the negative, to turn it around, to learn from it, and to capitalize on it. From them, I learned that if I strived to reach my potential and stayed true to my core beliefs, then I truly could become someone. I learned that the word "can't" is non-existent, and that only the weak and jealous will try to crush, diminish, or extinguish another's dreams. My family taught me that I am able to accomplish any goal or dream that I aspire to, and they continue to be my subconscious strength during challenging times.

To all of the people I have not mentioned, you are remembered in my heart and in the many stories I use in my work day after day.

Thank you,

Brad Pattison

Table of Contents

Chapter 1 - Puppy Overview

Chapter 2 – Toys and Play

Chapter 3 — Equipment

Chapter 4 — The Forbidden Zone

Chapter 5 — Hand-Friendly

Chapter 6 — Grooming

Chapter 11 – Street Safety Training

Chapter 12 – Five SUPER COOL Commands

Chapter 13 – Corrections

Introduction

The knowledge in this book is pure and raw. It contains proven training methods that work. There is no masking. There are no frills and no gimmicks. This book demands the utmost of your time and energy to successfully accomplish each training task.

Each lesson has valuable information that will guide you along the road to a better relationship with your dog.

Study, watch, and listen when working alongside any dog; whether it is your own or a clients'. Be patient, trust the dog, and remember that the learning curve will vary from chapter to chapter.

It's also important to remember that each breed is different, and that each dog within the breed has its own unique personality. This means that the length and intensity of the learning process will differ for every dog. However, if you are patient and set aside time daily to practice, I guarantee that the learning can be accomplished.

My knowledge on this subject is the result of the close working relationships I have shared with many dogs and their people over the years and my extensive training in martial arts, which taught me to be an observer of both dogs and humans.

I believe that understanding canine communication leads to a more effective training experience. My dogs, Dez and Max, served as canine-to-human interpreters, providing me with an amazing window, through which I could see how dogs think and communicate. By sharing this insight, you will have the ability to provide your dog with the happy, liberated, and safe life that they deserve and ultimately, this will lead to a great friendship with your dog.

Let me explain why I have called my approach a 'university'. I want to raise the bar for dog training and bring it up to a level consistent with the concept of 'higher learning'. My belief is that the ultimate goal in dog training is an educated, well-rounded dog (the canine equivalent of a university degree).

No doubt you have a dog because you want a relationship with him. But if you didn't know much about dogs before you took the plunge, you may be starting to realize that the relationship you have is much different than the one you had imagined. It is my belief that you can have a better, more balanced relationship with your dog, once you give up your preconceived notions in favour of a little common sense.

Over the years, I have come to suspect that many people get dogs to fulfill a variety of needs that have nothing to do with owning a pet. While it's understandable that people have needs they seek to fulfill through a relationship with their dog, it is not fair to the animal. A principle that I stand by is that a dog's birthright is to be a dog.

It is therefore your responsibility to recognize what a privilege it is to share your life with a dog. Honour the inter-species relationship and respect what it means for our dogs to be dogs and to live a canine life. When a dog is free to be a dog, (and I must emphasize in the ways that are compatible with living in human society), the dog is happier, and with appropriate training, is better behaved.

By treating your dog like a dog, you can learn to have fun with him in a way that you never imagined. I encourage you to commit to this kind of training: Your hard work and perseverance will be rewarded immeasurably.

I frequently become involved with clients and their dogs after they have worked with numerous trainers (sometimes as many as four or more) without success. By this time the dog is older, optimal training time is running out, and the dog must unlearn bad habits in order to learn good ones. This is not a great place to start; yet I do find success where other trainers haven't. I believe this is because, for me, dog training is a vocation - not a job. I care about the dog and work to focus everyone involved on the education and the well being of that dog. My approach is results-oriented rather than time and activity based, and I always stand by my results.

Dog training is relationship based. It is a partnership. It is impossible for the dog to learn on its' own. It must be recognized, that a lack of knowledge on the owner's part can contribute to the development of bad habits in the dog but, I don't expect clients to come pre-equipped with a high-level of dog training knowledge. I do however, expect them to seek to learn. It is essential for clients to commit to the education and development of a positive relationship with their dog.

"Control" is a loaded word when it comes to dogs. Clearly we have an expectation, both socially and legally, that owners should have their dogs under control at all times. But what does 'under control' mean? Too often, owners forgo appropriate off-leash training and substitute actual control for the illusion of it by using the leash, thinking that this is how to have their dog under complete control. Many obedience schools never progress beyond leash training.

This, in my opinion, fails to adequately train the dog. Dogs need to be able to play off-leash and to know how to conduct themselves appropriately. It is misguided to think that you can control every situation. Accidents happen. Gates and doors get left open unintentionally. Your dog needs to know how to behave off his leash for everyone's welfare, including his own.

Unfortunately, too many people get a dog without realizing how much work will be involved. I will not work with a client who is not fully committed. While this is painful for me when I consider the dog, it would be a futile exercise to attempt the training without this crucial commitment from the owner.

Amazingly, I get requests to take the dog, train it, and give it back to the owner. Not only does this speak to their complete lack of commitment, but also to their lack of understanding about how to build a partnership and relationship. While I have taken dogs into my home and trained them, it has always been with the significant involvement of the owners. This is to both reinforce their relationship on the same basis as I have with their dog, and to maintain continuity of training after their transition back into the home.

Another reason for writing this book is to share my philosophy of 'positive dog training'. By positive, I mean thinking positively and expecting positive results. What I am talking about is making a 'self fulfilling prophecy' work to your dog's advantage. If you expect positive results, it is more likely that your dog will meet your expectations. This is what is meant by "Be surprised when your dog does something wrong, not when it does something right." If you and your dog are communicating and enjoying a good relationship, your praise should be enough encouragement. Within my framework for positive training, I have given the dog the benefit of the doubt, and the result has been favourable. Why not try it with your dog, and modify what hasn't been working?

I also do not subscribe to most of the accepted beliefs about how dogs process and recall information. In working with dogs, I have seen them learn in situations and in ways that experts would say was impossible. I have concluded that there is a lot of misconception masquerading as fact. We are just beginning to develop a body of knowledge about our canine friends, and there is much left to learn.

Finally, know that overnight success is not possible with dog training, or any other type of learning. I encourage you to work hard, be tenacious, to persevere and always strive for excellence.

Here's to friends of a different kind!

Chapter 1

Puppy Overview

Welcoming Your New Puppy

Can a few weeks make a difference?

A breeder's error can cause you hundreds, even thousands of dollars in damages, not to mention incredible frustration.

Every puppy I have worked with in the past twelve years that was removed from the litter between 6 and 7 weeks, was destructive and suffered from separation anxiety. Puppies that were removed even slightly before the 8 week challenged their human parents more than a pup that was weaned properly and stayed with its Mom past eight weeks.

I once worked with siblings from two different human families. One family picked up their pup at 7 weeks, and the other couple picked up their pup at 8 1/2 weeks. The puppy that was removed earlier, even though it was just a few days difference, chewed more shoes, destroyed more furniture, was more difficult to house train, and had quicker temper tantrums.

15

Thankfully, this puppy landed with a fantastic parent who was willing to put in the extra effort necessary to correct the imbalance.

When Should You Get Your Puppy?

When you find your puppy of choice and decide to collect your new "child", please do not remove the pup before 8 weeks. If at all possible, ask to collect your new pup at 9 weeks. If you have difficulties because the breeder won't allow this, then leave and find another breeder that will.

Owning a dog is a big responsibility, and I am sure you are going to do the best you know how in raising it. Start off with a pup that has been raised by its Mom for the correct amount of time.

These early weeks are critical to your puppy's growth and development. They lay the foundation that will help your puppy grow into a happy, healthy and socially well-adjusted dog. No human being can replace the learning and nurturing a puppy receives from its Mother. Please do not rob your new puppy of this important learning and enjoyment, just because you are anxious to get it home. The puppy will still be just as cute, cuddly and small at 9 weeks.

CONGRATULATIONS!...

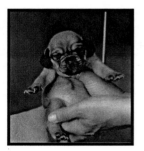

"Oh My Gosh - Look at the puppy!"

How many times have you heard that as a dog owner?
Listen to people and the way they address their dogs. Listen to their vocal tone. What does it sound like? Say it to yourself three times. Is the voice high pitched and whiny? Is the voice coming from the throat or chest?
Is it coming from the bottom of the stomach?

16

More than likely, their voice is coming from the mouth and no further than the throat. We often hear people speaking to babies in the same manner. Your words are not saying hello to your puppy, but your tone certainly is. Dogs are not born bilingual. They seek out vocal tone and smells well before they understand our words.

"The rate at which a puppy learns is far quicker than that of a human child."

What does this really mean in the big picture?

There is no time to procrastinate in training the new puppy!

You are the Alpha and the puppy is not. No ifs, ands, or buts.

Limit the amount of damage a puppy will cause by demanding and expecting a standard of behaviour that suits your lifestyle.

Puppies will destroy property left, right, and center if guidance and rules are not in place from the beginning. Can you eliminate all bad incidents and destructive behaviour? No, but you can minimize the damage and the number of items that have been chewed up and spat out.

Feeding Your Puppy

A balanced diet for your dog is very important Just like us, dogs need protein in their diets. Unlike us, however, they need a lot more of it. Lamb is richer meat compared to beef or fish. Depending on the breed, chicken is usually the better choice. 28% protein is average in dry puppy foods. If you have a larger breed, change the food to adult or mix in half and half. Or feed the higher protein meal to the puppy in the morning if you're doing more exercise during the day, and then feed a lower protein meal in the evening. A small difference goes a long way. The higher the amount of protein, the more energy your dog will have.

Soft canned food has always made me giggle. Read the ingredients. There is a whole lot of water and not a lot of quality nutrition. Now that doesn't mean that all canned foods are a waste of money. There are some good ones out there, but you'll need to look around (read the ingredient lists). Canned food for puppies is not something I promote. Your puppy has sharp little teeth that hurt as they grow in, so a good hard crunchy food is what they need. Consult your Veterinarian on which kind of food is best for your pup.

Water, water and more water! A bowl filled with water will always satisfy your puppy, either for quenching its thirst or for having a wee bit of a birdbath in! Make sure your puppy or dog always has access to fresh water. On the road, you can bring a water bottle along and pour the water into a collapsible water dish (these are widely available at both pet and large Big Box stores) at each stop.

We have been brought up to believe that the dog food you start with is the dog food you end with. Welcome to healthy eating for your pet: For as long as I have owned dogs, I have never stuck with one flavour or one brand. As each bag becomes empty, I purchase a different flavour from a different brand name to offer variety to my dog. I will feed chicken and rice this month. Next month, I might feed lamb and rice. I could never imagine how boring and awful eating would be without variety.

To illustrate this further, let's imagine you are served potatoes and beans for every meal over a one year period. You're probably already imagining how yucky that would taste. Suddenly, a carrot muffin appears! You love the taste of it so much, and you inhale it at such a rate that there is no time for chewing. You feel pretty darn good because a completely different food taste was presented to you, don't you? The next day, you are visiting the

bathroom a little more frequently than the previous day, and the situation is a little runnier than on previous visits. Do you have food poisoning? Of course not, you fed your body a different nutritional food substance, and your body reacted accordingly. Are you never going to eat another carrot muffin? No, you will eat many more because you enjoyed the taste. And as you eat more carrot muffins, your body will adjust, and the "runs" will return to being about your son's baseball team.

But so many Moms and Dads STILL insist on feeding their dogs one type of food, half for convenience and half because they think it's better for their pets. Is it? Well, let's think about this: Your dog needs balanced nutrition every day. To me, that means changing the ingredient list to achieve the "balance".

Look at what you eat. Your meals are constantly changing. WHY? Because you want to eat a wide variety of ingredients so you can achieve nutritional balance. Do the same for your dog, and watch for his smile.

19

Where to Sleep

When a puppy is introduced to the new home where it will be raised, it needs to be shown where he/she is going to sleep. There are a broad range of locations for dogs' sleeping areas that include sleeping outdoors in an open yard, being confined in a dog run, being isolated in a crate or portable kennel, dog house, blanket, dog bed, closet, or under a bed.

Whose is whose?

Your bed is yours, not your dog's. A dog bed, crate, or other designated area is the dog's. What is yours is not the dog's. What is the dog's, however, can be yours.

Sleeping arrangements can communicate who the Alpha is to a dog.

When you are Alpha, the dog thinks, "I understand that you are my leader, I will listen and obey the rules that are placed before me. I see consistency in my eating, who I follow, and where I sleep." Laying the foundation at an early stage (when the dog enters your home) will lessen later confrontation and give clarity to your dog.

Remember: Your bed is yours only, not for both you and your dog.

This is the rule as you start to establish your Alpha status in your dog's life.
(Learn how in Chapter 7 Establishing Alpha)

So, what's the harm in letting our dog snuggle on our bed, every now and then?

A dog's aggressive behaviour can ignite over jealousy, territory protection, or simple selfishness; "I don't want to share". The outcome of various attitudes can range from a simple growl to a serious dog bite. A high percentage of dogs who stake claims on beds, and who also have the run of the house, are territorially aggressive.

This means that if your dog feels like it is entitled to the beds in your house, and a child tries to get him/her off of one, there's a good chance that that child will get bit (because the dog is aggressive about its own territory).

Teach your dog not to go on the beds!

What Signals Are You Sending to Your Dog?

A client of mine always cuddled with her dog. Her dog sat on her lap, and often walked on her desk while she was at work. The dog was carried to the car and completely pampered. Is this a crime? No, not really, but it is a way to love your dog to death.

Over petting, cuddling constantly, squeezing, and picking them up are a few examples of how you can create a co-dependent relationship with your dog.

When Mom left the office and left the dog behind, the dog would pee on the carpet, whine profusely, bark, or have a conniption and destroy things. The dog would also hop up on the desk and urinate and defecate on her paper work.

Where does this unacceptable tantrum behaviour come from? Dogs will test each situation that arises. An example would be jumping up, or trying to climb someone's leg. This type of behaviour is common in all puppies, however if you allow them to get away with it, then they will test you in other ways. For example, people let their dog sit on their lap while they are eating, and the dog learns to beg for food.

Here's another example: Your sweet, cuddly puppy exits or enters your home before you, walking through the door while you follow. Suddenly he begins to think he is above you in rank. With each situation presented before the dog above, the owner's body language granted the dog permission to do as he pleased.

What does this mean exactly in the eyes of your innocent, quick-learning puppy?

Your puppy was born as a pack animal, regardless of the breed. In the pack, each puppy is responsible for fighting for food from the Mom. Within a few weeks, it is easy to see who the fastest growing puppy is.

Soon, we are able to observe who will feed the most and who will feed the least. A runt in the litter is often the smallest for various reasons: birth placement, possibly last born in the litter, born weaker, not enough nipples to feed from, or it might be slower to get to the nipple for feeding.

With each challenge a puppy successfully overcomes comes strength, confidence, and the knowledge of where it stands amongst its siblings.

Puppies gain a lot of knowledge in a very short period of time (just a few weeks). Over the next five weeks of its life, we can observe personalities forming. Watching, following, and imitating Mom is a daily occupation for each puppy.

As the puppies become stronger, wrestling matches fall into a common training game that is played out over and over. "Catch me if you can" and "I'm going to chew on a body part", are some of the games they play. These games form the basic learning tools that are promoted, not discouraged, by Mom. She oversees them, ensuring they are playing within the rules.

For example, if one puppy continuously chews on a lower-ranked sibling, and the lower ranked sibling verbally expresses the pain, Mom will notice that the higher ranked sibling is not abiding by the rules of consideration. She will then step in and verbally break up the two. Once a puppy verbally expresses, "Hey! that hurt", with a high-pitched squeak, the playmate will let go. You will then usually see each dog shake itself off, and play will resume.

When you bring your new furry friend home, you take the place of the puppy's Mom. The puppy is no longer socializing with its siblings, or its birth mother. The puppy, which played throughout the day, is now alone. Instead of being paid attention to through wrestling and cuddling, she is being picked up and held against your chest, and her movement is restricted.

We all have a fear that the little puppy we are now responsible for might get hurt. So we justify this by holding and carrying the puppy.

As a parent, you need to allow your puppy to be a puppy, and let them explore and seek out the millions of tastes, smells and experiences it needs to build his knowledge of the world around him. It's the equivalent of you or I reading the paper.

23

When you clutch your puppy in your arms every time a dog comes around, you are taking away an incredible social learning experience.

Allow your puppy to say hello and to play with as many dogs as possible.

You can learn much about your dog through these interactions. Look at the tail positioning. How is the head held? Is it up, or is it lowered? Does your dog have a smile, or is he or she running scared? While all of this activity is going on, your dog is maturing, and the social skills are being enhanced and critiqued by other dogs.

In the long run, that means you will have a better and more socialized dog.

Good Rules to Implement

- You lead on stairs.
- The puppy follows you entering or exiting the house.
- You walk first through any doorway, including gates.
- You eat meals first, the puppy second.

Keep Your Puppy Off:

Couches, beds, tables, chairs
Your lap when driving a vehicle
Your lap when sitting on couches etc.

An example of what NOT to do!

No Jumping Up On:

You, strangers, children, friends and family
The edge of the couch, side of your bed and the outside door

If you expect your dog to abide by all of these rules, then you need to do something for your puppy.

You need to get down on your hands and knees and play the way two puppies would play together. This is quite important. It builds your dog's trust, love, and confidence.

Your dog learns life skills in what is acceptable with humans, and also builds an incredibly strong bond between you and her.

Exposing your puppy to all sorts of different activities as you live your life day-to-day; while setting boundaries, will teach your dog more than if you leave the little fur ball locked up all the time.

Setting guidelines and a structured living situation only benefits your puppy in the long run.

Potty Training

Friend: *"Hey your dog pooped in my living room"*

Dog Owner *"Sorry, I guess he did"*

Friend *"Well aren't you going to discipline him?"*

Dog Owner *"No! Why should I, he doesn't remember he went to the bathroom."*

A bowel movement is a natural act, but your dog needs to be shown where and when it is appropriate to be done. As with little children, dogs need structure in order to learn well.

Here's how to "potty train" your dog:

The most appropriate time to begin this type of training is first thing in the morning.

Put your pet on a 6ft leash and direct the dog to the designated area. This can be a dog run, an out-of-sight place in the yard, or in a dog litter box. Speak calmly to your dog while walking to the designated spot. Your responsibility is to hold the leash and to keep the dog in the area that you have chosen. Allow the dog to sniff the ground, and allow ample slack in the leash so he doesn't feel restricted while getting into position. When he's sniffing the ground, say "go pee pee" or "go poo poo" to your dog (and try not to think about your neighbours listening in…).

Wait until your dog begins to go pee, and then address the dog and praise him/her with "good pee pee".

Pat your dog on the head and give him good strong praise with physical touch. Next, the dog needs to finish up with the "poo poo" part. Allow him to re-position himself to accommodate the next task.

Upright Poop Position

Okay, now say, "go poo poo," along with the dog's name. Allow him to find the best spot in the designated area. When the dog has taken up the pooping position, quietly praise him, but do not touch him at this time.

When he/she is finished, praise in the same manner as with the pee experience. Finally, walk your dog back into the house and go make your latte.

Male Marking Pole

Take your dog out, following the routine above, after eating, exercising, and at regular intervals throughout the next week. Take note of his habits: does he go out 4 times per day? What body language does he show to indicate that he needs to pee or poo? When does he go?

Once you know his routine and body language, you can take him to the designated pee spot at the times when you expect that he will need to go.

Remember: Praise him with the "potty words" every time he succeeds.

Happy training!

27

Questions

- What are the commands to address the dog?
- When is the best time to begin this training?
- Does a dog empty the bladder first?

How should you handle a potty-training mistake?

O.K., so you just found a deposit on the floor, and it's been there for a day or two. Do you still discipline your dog? Many of you will answer NO, that you cannot. Unfortunately, that's the wrong answer. Many trainers disagree with this, and I haven't figured out why yet. If

Pavlov's dog was able to show the world that dogs can remember things, why do we think that they will not remember that they have gone to the bathroom in the house?

If you clean up the mess and carry on with life, you will be encouraging your puppy to repeat the same naughty behaviour. Rather, once you find the "gift" that your puppy has deposited, call him back to the site.

Now sit on the floor and talk to your puppy, asking if this was the right thing to do (using a conversational tone). This conversation should last at least one minute.

Do not grab your puppy in a harsh way, but do show your puppy the mistake. Hook your index finger between the collar and the neck while you're doing this, and do not allow your puppy to argue back. If your puppy displays an attitude towards you and this situation, then pin her to the ground (see page 84 how to pin your dog). Wait until the puppy has settled, then continue your conversation with an even vocal tone, making your puppy look at the mistake.

Now carry on with your daily activities, but do not have conversation with your puppy for fifteen minutes. No eye contact either.

Another option is to put her outside. I do not suggest this option often, though, because the yard is usually a place where the puppy gets to enjoy and have fun.

The silent treatment and lack of interaction is very strong discipline. Remember, body language speaks louder than words to puppies.

Terrible Twos

The "Terrible Twos" are usually the most difficult period for both the owner and the puppy.

Between the ages of seven and ten months, the puppy enters into a stage where they sometimes become destructive and they suddenly seem to forget everything they have been taught.

Quite possibly, this is just a naturally occurring stage, and the dog isn't actually choosing to drive you mad. I don't know if there is scientific evidence to explain this observation, but after twelve years of experience and thousands of canine students, I watch for the "Terrible Twos".

In my experience, every dog showed a sudden personality change when they hit this age range. Many puppies that have been taught in my Street Safety Classes have proven this fact over and over again.

Let me give you an example. A puppy may come to the first class at the age of six months. At about the seventh month, both the owner and I notice a difference in the dog's attention span. The puppy appears zoned out (as if he has tried "puppy weed"). Suddenly, it does not pay attention to its owner or show any enthusiasm about learning.

When I compared the dog's behaviour at this age to his behaviour in the previous classes, I always found significant changes.

For example, a Belgian sheep dog had learned hand signals for sit, stay, come, and stop at the age of five months. At eight months, it suddenly had no clue what the signals meant.

When the parents called to ask what possibly could have gone wrong, I asked them to join in the active class that was currently underway, as a "refresher". That way I would be able to critique any mistakes that might be

contributing to the dog's change in behaviour. The few mistakes they were making were so minute, that I didn't think they could be the cause of such a significant shift in the dog's behaviour.

Three weeks later, however, the dog pulled a 180-degree turn and was back on- course, responding effortlessly to training and was once again a gem to be with.

One of the characteristics of the Terrible Twos stage is a lack of acknowledgement when the dog is asked to do a basic task, such as sitting.

30

A five-minute sit-stay that was once easy is now next to impossible. A thirty minute stay is out of the question. Barking, running away, defecating in the house, chewing your belongings, challenging your Alpha position, and pulling on the leash when the dog should be heeling are all characteristics of the Terrible Twos .

This stage may last from a few days to a couple of months, and no, you can't ship them off to your parent's house for the entire time.

When your dog is in the Terrible Twos, keep in mind that two days before and after a full moon, your dog will be affected the most. If you live near the ocean and there is an extreme tide plus the full moon, then your dog's behaviour will be off-kilter more so than with just a full moon. (Hence, why I refer to this stage as "wacky")

.

When I had the dog day care, sometimes we would notice a significant behaviour change in as many as 25 dogs at a time. If the full moon fell on a Wednesday, then on Monday, the dogs would enter the daycare and play uncontrollably. They would have more energy, and this would usually last all day. On Tuesday, the dogs attending day care would simply say "hi" to one another, and then fall asleep immediately after entering in the morning. On the day of the full moon, the dogs would often become nasty with one another, and they would socialize with dogs that had never interested them in the past.

Unfortunately, the full moon affects a dog in the Terrible Two stage even more, sometimes causing tempers to flare.

Dogs may fall at the other end of the spectrum and be calmer during this stage, but there will still be a marked change in their behaviour. Many dogs that enter the Terrible Twos should not be permitted off-lead, as their reactions to situations are far too unpredictable.

31

My dog care parents (whose dogs were in their Terrible Twos), were always informed whether they should allow their dog to be off-leash, and what they might expect behaviour-wise. Patience is certainly an important factor when dealing with your dog in the Terrible Twos.

Some parents give up on training because they find it frustrating. We, as parents of a canine, however, have accepted a responsibility to care for and raise our puppies to be accountable and kind.

The puppy/dog will not give up, although it may appear like it will. But remember, your four-legged pet is going through a tough time, and he depends on you for everything. Do not dump on your dog because you're being challenged.

If you think you have it hard, place yourself in his paws. Breathe deeply and take it one day at a time. Your dog doesn't return you to the human pound during your phase of eating chocolate and yelling at phone solicitors all day!

The bottom line is this:

The dog didn't choose you - you chose the dog. Guide, communicate, and most of all, try to be understanding and take each day as it comes.

Socialization

Introduce your dog to as many dogs as possible at an early age. Introducing your dog to various age groups is also important. This teaches her about respect and taking on certain roles, such as parent or sibling type roles, as well as boyfriend, girlfriend, and best buddies.

This is all going to help round out your dog to be educated about various behaviours, and it also enhances the dog's social skills in body language and verbal communication with other dogs.

In addition to socializing your dog around other dogs, try to bring her into many different social situations while she is still a puppy.

Here are a few ideas: You can walk her in busy places (through a crowd), across an overpass bridge's sidewalk, through a group of children, and on different walking routes around your neighbourhood.

Be creative. The more your puppy sees and experiences when she is small, the more well rounded and confident she will be as adult dog.

PREPARING FOR TRAINING

This stuff is COOL to learn

7 Basic Commands

"Sit"
"Now"
"Stay"
"Heel",
"Come"
"Hustle",
"Relax"

Basic commands have one purpose: to get the dog to do something. When you ask the dog to sit, for example, the dog should obey and sit down. People unfortunately acquire bad habits along the way, and instead of saying the command once, they will ask the dog again and again. When this happens, the command loses meaning in the dog's eyes, and he gains the advantage in the training process.

More dogs than I care to speak of would be alive today if their owners' dog trainers had taught their clients not to repeat commands.

Basic commands are essential to ensure both your dog's safety, as well as that of other dogs and/or people in the park or out on the street. You need to be diligent in your responsibility as a canine parent. Watch for the unexpected, and be ready to steer your dog away from any potential hazard with these new helpful commands.

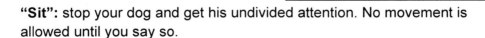

7 basic commands:
Come, Sit, Stay, Relax, Hustle, Heel, and Now.

"Come": use it to get your dog to catch up to you quickly.

"Sit": stop your dog and get his undivided attention. No movement is allowed until you say so.

"Stay": is stating that the dog is to do nothing but stay focused on you and your next request. The dog is not allowed to venture off and socialize. Even if another dog comes to say "hello", your dog does not move.

"Relax": this is a great word to educate your dog with. This is the word you need to use when animosity is building between two or more dogs, and you want your dog to submit and not to be the aggressor. When using this word, you are now expected to be the enforcer and aggressor if a situation breaks out.

"Hustle": Your dog responds to this word and drops what he is doing, and immediately pursues you.

"Now": This word is used in situations where the dog is being lackadaisical in their movement or response to a command you have just given them. Use this command with a very firm, strong and deep tone.

"Heel": Simple and straight forward, your dog takes up a side your right or left you with eye position, either on side, acknowledging contact.

I wish my Trainer would teach Mom & Dad that it's OK for me to have a personality!

Chapter 2

Toys & Play

So Many Toys!

So many colors, so many of "this" and so many of "that"…

I am always surprised by the amount of money owners waste purchasing incorrect toys!

When I am conducting my Street Safety Course, I ask clients what toys they have purchased for their dogs. Many are happy to blurt out the name of the latest ridiculous gadget they have just wasted their money on.

All dogs need a few good toys to play with; emphasis on "few". Three well chosen toys is all your dog really needs. Don't spoil your dog with abundance!

So here is one alternative to think about:

How about tying up an old t-shirt in a knot (so it doesn't look like any of your new ones) and play tug with your puppy?

Allow the puppy to fall in love with its new toy.

There are three reasons why this old t-shirt is better than the new toy.

1. It smells like you.
2. It's fun.
3. It feels great on your dog's teeth.

Safe Toys

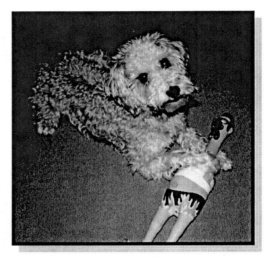

Are all toys safe and harmless? No!

Pet stores carry an abundance of toys that come in fancy colors and interesting shapes. Big and small, soft and hard, bouncy, noisy and sometimes annoying...most of these things are just plain useless. Don't assume, just because it's sold in a pet store that it is a safe or appropriate toy for your pet.

So, what is a safe toy?

First, look for toys that can withstand powerful jaws and sharp claws. This is important. Durability and a long life span are also characteristics of good toys.

A great toy on the market is the Kong. It's shaped like a beehive. It has thick durable rubber. It is safe for teeth and it does not peel or break apart. The Kong also comes in a variety of colors. For water lovers, purchase the blue and white Kong, as it is designed for water use because it floats. The other Kongs will sink to the bottom of the pond.

Plush toys and stuffed animals come in pretty much every color or animal design under the sun. When buying a plush toy, find one that is made with thick material. The thicker the material, the longer it will last. Remember, it needs to withstand the rugged play dogs will dish out.

Bones that have bone marrow in them make an excellent gnawing toy. They are fairly durable, but they will break down with wear and tear. Watch for parts beginning to break off and discard the bone when they do.

Soft Frisbees are wonderful toys for the dog that loves to play fetch.

When choosing balls for your dog, be careful to choose ones that are large enough so they will not get lodged in your dog's throat. Also, go for rubber balls that are sturdy enough to withstand canine teeth. To size up a ball for the correct size, do this: If the ball can be compressed and fit past the half way point in your dog's mouth, then it is too small

Here is a list of approved toys:

> Rope toys
> Kong
> Rubber balls
> Soft Frisbees
> Plush toys
> Towels
> Squeaky rubber toys
> Nyla bones

Approved toys must be sized according to the level of the dog's aggression and the size of her mouth versus the size of the toy.

39

Unsafe Toys

Tennis balls are one of the most overrated toys in the toy box. These widely sold balls can cause significant damage to teeth. Imagine brushing your teeth with a nail file. Would you? No. Tennis balls are wrapped with a felt that is as abrasive as a nail file, and over time, a dog's teeth will fall victim to the wear and tear they inflict. Dogs of all breeds are falling victim to premature wear and tear on their teeth. To avoid adding to this problem, never introduce tennis balls to your dog.

Plush toys that have plastic eyes are not safe because they can easily be removed. Consumption of plastic eyes is not only dangerous, it's just plain icky. Also, do not allow your dog to eat the stuffing from plush toys. Don't buy toys with frilly attachments. If you think that you can rip apart any of your dog's toys, just throw them out.

Remember that his jaws and gnawing determination are way more powerful than your hands. Give a toy the "yank and tear test": take two adults, have each of them grab one end of a toy and pull, pull hard, as hard as two people can. If the toy breaks, don't buy it.

Hard plastic Frisbees are also a definite no-no; this is a high-risk toy that can damage teeth.

Rawhide chew toys swell when they become very wet from saliva. Torn pieces of rawhide have been known to lodge inside a dog after being ingested, clogging the digestive tract and causing serious health problems. For this reason, it is not recommended to purchase rawhide bones *ever*.

Remember that common sense is your best friend when it comes to toys.

Here is the list of toys that I do NOT approve of:

- Tennis balls
- Rawhide bones that splinter
- Hard Frisbees
- Toys that are expired, torn, falling apart, or have insides that are exposed.

Tip: Take your dog to the pet store, throw a bunch of toys on the ground, and let go of the leash so your dog can relax and focus on playing with the toys. Walk a few feet away from your dog, not making eye contact. He'll be able to tell you which ones he wants in a hurry!

Learning Motor Mechanics

When puppies use their paws and mouths, they become more competent at motor mechanics. Toys play an important role in developing these, in paw to eye coordination, control, as well as developing the ability to grasp and clutch bones, sticks, and other toys. Perhaps most importantly, puppies gain confidence through playing with their toys.

41

Your Role in Toyland

Why is human interaction vital in your dogs life and what makes your playtime so valuable?

Simple - we all like friends, and we all like to play.

Dogs are social animals and they have socialization needs to be met. When a human interacts with a dog, the dog pays attention.

If we introduce our dog to a toy that he likes, then his behaviour will change. This behaviour change will be different than during a conversation or when he is receiving pats on the head. When dogs react during play, they are communicating that they would like to play, tug, fetch, chase, etc.

All of these activities require at least two involved individuals: one being you and the other being the dog. The dog naturally wants to develop his interactive social skills and playtime is very beneficial for this. Respect, honour, bonding, belonging to a pack, and communication are all pertinent to the development of a well-rounded dog. Dogs learn many of these foundation skills through play.

A dog will follow the rules that you set during your playtime, and he will see the toy as his reward.

Your pet may bring you a toy when you are sitting down watching television or reading a book. Ignoring his invitation to play can be damaging to your dog. He may go into a state of depression and sulk. Your responsibility is to acknowledge the dog's presence and the fact that the dog is physically asking you to play. You need to respond verbally, letting him know that playtime is not now, but that you will play later. Non- verbal or non-  communicative body language is an inconsiderate way to treat your dog.

Chapter 3

Equipment

Leashes

Leashes have one main purpose - to keep the dog attached to you. This purpose is simple and fairly straight forward, but having said that, there are still some issues to consider when walking your dog on-lead.

A leash is the tie between you and your dog, an extension of your hand that keeps your dog within your control. Are there some leashes on the market that are better than others? Yes, but that all depends on what your expectations are.

Heeling leads, or short leads, range from 1 to 4 ft in length and are confining and limiting to a dog's behaviour.
The long-term effects when using such leads are often your dog's anxiety and resentment while on a walk.

Your leash needs to complement, assist, guide, and be a part of a positive experience for your dog. When your dog sees his leash, we want him to think, "GREAT! Let's go for a walk!", and not, "OH NO! We're going for a walk."

Caution needs to be used if there is too much freedom granted prematurely, such as leashes that extend to a length greater than six feet. This instils a false sense of security because the dog is attached to something. There are many dangers  associated with too long a leash. I have seen homemade leashes that are up to fifty feet long that offer no real control, other than finally stopping the dog at fifty feet, when there is no other choice. This is definitely not control.

Personally, I prefer a 6ft long leash that is made out of good quality nylon that is three-quarters of an inch to one inch in width. This is your best choice  unless you are doing tracking, search and rescue, or animal control with a working breed. Other than that, there is no reason not to use a 6ft lead. Remember, unless you are doing specific training, there is no need to have an assortment of leashes.

Note that some leather leashes may be poorly dyed, and the dye may bleed out onto fabric or skin when wet. Leather leashes can also stretch over time if the dog pulls frequently.

The clasp on your lead should also be made of good quality material. Make sure the spring mechanism inside the clasp is good quality, as it is very important to keep the clasp closed and securely attached to the collar.

44

When looking at clasps, look for a stiff movement or a strong pinch to show that the clasp is securely closed.

Collars

A good quality collar works in conjunction with a good quality leash to ensure that your dog is safe while on-lead. There are many types of collars that come in a variety of colors, shapes, and sizes. So, how do you select the correct collar for your dog?

First, we look at the needs of the dog, which is for you to have control while handling him. You need a collar that reacts quickly and smoothly, when making corrections, but is also humane. Control, safety, and comfort are key ingredients to look for when selecting an appropriate collar.

Note: Even if you are a movie star in LA, this next section still applies to you.

Hustle Up™ Collar

www.bradpattison.com

Fashionable collars are great to look at, but are not very versatile. When you have spent the time needed to educate your dog, a fashionable collar is fun to wear. However, as a training collar, they are not very useful and generally not a good idea.

The leash and collar are the two most important training tools you will need to train your dog correctly. But *(and unfortunately it is a big "but")* on the market, there are also a wide variety of useless training tools available.

I do not believe in collars that inflict pain or that cause anguish and stress. I do not believe in choke chains or pinch collars, as I find them to be extremely harmful to a dog's physical and mental well-being. Inflicting continuous pain while on a basic walk is simply cruel and certainly not

45

constructive. If you are considering this type of collar for your dog, think of it being used on yourself. I guarantee that you will have a different perspective on the equipment you purchase for your dog!

Personally, I would like to see pinch collars and choke chains banned from the market permanently!

When I correct a dog, I need a crisp, quick movement that is non-restricting. I need a collar that works with positive results, not short cuts or cover-ups, and I don't want a collar that conditions a dog to the corrections. The only collar I endorse using is the Martingale Collar, which has met every expectation of mine as a dog behaviourist. All other collars have failed me, often more than once. If the collar fails, I am in a losing situation with whatever dog I may be working with. I need to trust the collar and be confident that it will meet my needs and expectations.

Keep in mind that all MARTINGALE Collars are not made with the same quality of materials, but they may be very similarly designed and made with the same basic working mechanics. When you purchase one for medium and large breeds, it is imperative that the collar meet the highest possible standards in craftsmanship and quality. A collar that breaks on you is not a good tool. There are both poor quality and great quality products out there, so when buying your dog's collar, be sure to purchase one that will meet your demands.

When purchasing a collar, you will need to consider friction, stress, washing, and the climate you live in (harsh winters, humidity etc) to ensure you make the best choice.

The working chain needs to be able to handle the force dogs exert when pulling, as well as the regular wear and tear it will endure. If you are using a collar with a plastic clasp, check it periodically to see if cracks are forming or if the plastic is wearing down. The life span on plastic collars can be very short if you compare it to buckle collars or the MARTINGALE Collar.

On the metal loops of choke collars or the MARTINGALE, always check the big metal ring to see if there is any separation at the weld.

46

The threading on nylon, leather, or fabric collars should also be checked periodically to ensure that the collar will not fall apart while on a walk. When you consider all the options, however, your best bet is still the MARTINGALE Collar and a six-foot nylon leash. Hustle Up™ brand Martingale collars may be purchased online at www.bradpattison.com.

Beds

Bedding is usually chosen based on appearance. However, when selecting a bed for your dog, your focus *should* be on putting your dog's needs first and your interior decorating concerns second. Forget about what you like or want, or how it may look.

Consider the following list as a guideline to help you choose the correct bed for your dog:

- Where will the dog be sleeping, indoors or outdoors?
- Is the dog coat short or long?
- How many distinct seasons are there where you live?
- What are the temperature ranges?
- What type of floor will be under the dog's bed, carpet, concrete, dirt, hard wood floor, linoleum or tile?
- Will the dog be sleeping under your bed, in a doghouse, on a wooden porch, or on a grassy or snow-covered surface?
- If the dog is sleeping indoors, what is the room temperature?

Heavy insulation is not necessary in the case of hardwood flooring or carpet. However, in the case of concrete, dirt, linoleum, or tile, where the floor's temperature can dip below the room's temperature, it is advisable to have a heat barrier separating the bed from the ground, to keep the warmth in the bed. This barrier will also keep moisture away from the dog's bed. Below sixty degrees Fahrenheit, it is advisable to have the bed either elevated above the ground or well insulated. In the case of a doghouse on the ground or with a wooden floor, an old blanket and/or straw can be used as insulation, with the bed on top.

When shopping for a bed, keep maintenance in mind: washable fabric makes cleaning easy and of course a zipper helps. Bedding for your dog can be filled with Styrofoam pellets, cedar, or a foam mix. The size of the bed should be larger than the dog, with at least a six-inch buffer around him. If purchasing a bed for a puppy, start with a large bed and let him grow into it. It's a better idea to save your money and buy one bed instead of three or four as the dog grows.

Crates

Crates are not only great for traveling, but are also a wonderful training tool. Many people purchase one oversized crate, so they don't need to worry about setting the dog up in a second or third one as it grows. But unlike the dog bed, this is not the best plan.

The problem is that the puppy has so much room in the gigantic crate, it can set up a kitchen, bathroom, and bedroom all in the same location. Now, the owner gets ticked-off because the crate is wet, stinky and has a gift near one of the corners. To avoid this situation, I advise you to either rent crates as the puppy grows, or buy larger crates as necessary (you can always sell them online or donate them to an animal shelter). Also, consult your pet store or veterinarian for any trade in or swapping programs they may have.

Chapter 4

The Forbidden Zone

> ➤ Who left the paw print pathway across the new couch?

> ➤ What does the term "my domain", mean to humans (think - your favourite chair)?

> ➤ Do you find yourself accidentally sitting on your dog when you finally sit down to relax?

> ➤ Did you recently splurge on an angora bedspread? Whoops! That's not angora; it's dog hair!

Your Domain – Their Domain

Your domain exists everywhere: your house, car, boat, camper, or your work place. Regardless of the breed or personality, there is always a way to teach them that your property is not theirs.

Do you allow your dog to poop or pee on the hallway carpet? I'm quite certain that you'd respond with a NO. Why? Because it's your domain! You live in this house. The carpet belongs to you, and you will forbid your dog to soil what you regard as your property.

We've already talked about the couch being for you to sit on, and not for the puppy to use.

Respecting each other's property falls between two jurisdictions, Canine and Human. You need to respect your dog's bed, and not stand on it or leave a pile of clothing covering his sleeping space.

Your dog is owner of their crate, if they have one. Their bed is theirs, as well as the bowl they eat out of.

The dog needs to be taught and corrected not to "repeat offend" when he does something wrong in your domain. When your belongings have encountered a mishap, regardless of whether you find out several minutes or

50

even days later, it is still important and relevant to address the issue with your dog.

Think about that for a moment when the next trainer tells you that your dog doesn't remember. That's just ridiculous! Does your dog remember where the park is, what a car ride means, or when his owner is coming home? Of course they do. So when anyone tells you that your dog is unable to remember, reconsider the facts. YOUR DOG HAS A BRAIN! We don't know precisely how their brain functions, but my experience in working with many dogs tells me that it pays to give them the benefit of the doubt.

Your favourite pair of shoes is a common item that ends up in dogs' mouths. No wait; to be more accurate, it is usually only one shoe that gets destroyed!

So if you find that a shoe has been gnawed, or completely destroyed, then your dog has not respected your property.

So how do you teach your dog what is yours and what is his or hers?

Praise your dog when they play with their designated toys, and speak to them in a deep tone when they become interested in your property.

Use one word or a sentence that lets them know that it is not theirs to chew or play with. Your word can be "NO", and your sentence can be "WHAT ARE YOU DOING?" or "I DON"T THINK THAT BELONGS TO YOU MISSY". Get creative and find what works for you.

Always replace your chewed belonging with something that belongs to the dog, and give it to the dog right away. Never allow the dog to continue to chew your belonging, and certainly *do not* place it in their toy box or allow them to have it at a later date.

It is crucial to be consistent!

Does your dog piddle on the crate when sleeping? Some dogs will. This is because it's new to them, and they have not yet grasped the concept of their "den". It may be that they still believe it is yours, or they are unable to hold their movements. It could also be that you have put your dog in a crate that is too big. (see page 48). In time, the dog will learn that the crate is his safe haven from the outside world, including the house itself.

Use either a hand signal or a verbal command to direct your dog to his bed. This will solidify your dog's trust in you that it is a safe place that belongs to them. (refer to page 130 for how to teach "Bed")

Also, do not climb into their crate. I've heard of owners doing that before. You have no more right to be in their sleeping quarters then they have on your bed. Don't create a double standard. It becomes confusing to the dog.

Lap Dog Syndrome

So, what happens when owners don't teach fluffy to respect their domain?

Lap dog syndrome is responsible for any number of problems. I know of a small dog whose Mom cares very dearly for her delightful fur ball. However, she continuously allows and prompts her dog to sit and snuggle on her lap. Not surprisingly, when she has friends over, her dog is a nuisance to them. It jumps up into the lap of anyone

sitting down, knocking a drink (sometimes hot tea) out of a hand or otherwise being a genuine bother to her guests.

If a guest is sitting on the edge of the couch with a hand blocking the dog's efforts to jump, or is moving towards the dog as the dog attempts to jump up, the dog will not succeed on leaping up onto the lap. In protest, the dog runs around and barks at the person that did not oblige the dog's desire to be a lap dog.

This is one example of how an owner has moulded her dog's behaviour.

But, it gets even worse:

The owner then purchased a new sports car, and when she was driving around town, she decided that she didn't want her dog on her lap, so she pushed her dog onto the passenger seat. They struggled over the seats for a while, and when Mom finally said a firm "No" to her lap, her dog peed all over the leather seat, while looking her owner straight in the eye. The car was less than two days old!

This type of behaviour is very common, but it has other effects in addition to what I have just mentioned.

The same dog that urinated on the car seat also accomplished other destructive feats.

Mom had her boyfriend stay the night, and the dog antagonized them by leaping up onto the bed and barking continuously. She finally locked the dog out of the room and that *appeared* to work...

When morning came, however, she found all the houseplants dug up and shredded all over the carpet. Two piles of poop and three urine spots added to the mess. While she was cleaning up the carpet in the morning, the dog went to the bedroom and urinated on the bed!

All of this behaviour stems from allowing the dog free reign in the owner's domain. She had allowed cuddling on her lap on the couch, kitchen chair, in her bed, and at the office.

These few innocent cuddles led to thousands of dollars on clean up and repairs. To this day, this dog owner has not changed her habits and remains subordinate to her dog.

Understand this: when a dog, regardless of size or breed, is being carried or cuddled on top of you, you are transferring that Alpha status to the dog.

Consider how dogs view this situation in the wild: When two dogs are socializing, and one is always on top, that "top" dog is controlling the situation and is seen as the Alpha dog. He or she will remain the "top dog" unless there is a challenge.

Many of us forget that our small dogs are going to grow up to be big dogs, and that their learning curve is much more intense and short-lived compared to humans.

Why teach cute puppies bad habits that you will need to correct when they get to be older dogs? Teach your dog correctly right from the start, and avoid the need to over-correct all the time.

The Nasty Nylon Problem:

When my client Lisa called me, her goal was never to allow her dog to destroy one more pair of nylons. To ensure that Lisa was serious about this, she and I made a deal. For every pair of nylons her dog snagged while jumping up, she would pay me the equal amount for the cost of new nylons.

Of course I agreed to this only *after* I had given Lisa instructions on what to do when her dog wanted to jump up.

The day Lisa picked up her dog, she made sure that she was wearing a skirt. This was her reminder that the dog was not allowed to climb on her when she knelt down, nor was he allowed to jump on her when she was standing up.

Day one was a success. Lisa began calling me daily to tell me how her dog was developing and changing. What Lisa hadn't realized, was how she could read her dog by its body language, and how she could stop her dog verbally just as its' front paws were leaving the ground. She learned to notice her dog's body language in how her front legs would straighten, then bend, when she was just about to leap upwards. This was the exact moment when she spoke to her dog and said "Just a moment I'll pet you when I'm done."

It has now been over two years, and to this day her dog has not destroyed any more of her nylons, or sent any more of her clothes prematurely to the cleaners. She has not caused any damage to her friends' clothing either.

Needless to say, she worked hard and it paid off. Now her dog is always invited into people's homes because they know that her dog is well behaved. I didn't make any money from our agreement, which pleases me. Lisa applied herself as a responsible Mom, and her dog's success was her own success.

My oldest brother Kevin trained dogs in Massachusetts. At Christmas one year when I was visiting him, he said this to me...

55

"Don't be surprised when your dog does something right.
Be surprised when your dog does something wrong."
– Kevin Pattison

I pondered this phrase for a few years, and I was amazed at how much truth there was in it. Since hearing his words, dog training has taken on a completely new meaning for me.

I realized, when teaching, that if owners could address their dogs in a positive way, then they could create an easier learning space for the animals. I have explained to many people working with their dogs, that if you expect your dog to do wrong and make mistakes, then you will become accustomed to accepting failing behaviour. Why? A negative expectation starts training from the negative.

Of course you first need to show your dog what a "sit" is, for instance, before you ask him to do the task. However, once you have succeeded in teaching and showing your dog how to sit, then you expect your dog to sit. And as I mentioned, expect your dog to sit on command. Do not expect it not to sit.

Expect your dog to succeed, and he will!

The Couch

Ahh, the couch: the inevitable "second bed". Sweet cuddles, pleasant puppy breath, and your puppy drifts off into a deep sleep, all the while cradled in your arms while you're sitting on the smooth green leather. The phone rings and you lay the puppy on a cushion.

56

While on the phone, the puppy awakens and moves into the corner of the couch. You come back and stroke the puppy's head while watching television. Is this cozy scene harmful? YES it is! The puppy now knows that sleeping on the couch is okay.

Battles are fought over this famous piece of furniture. They want on: You want them off. Many of us have unfortunately pre-trained the puppy or dog to feel that the couch is equally theirs, so how can we blame them for wanting to stay on when our company arrives?

A great approach to teaching the pup that the couch is not a place for them, is by not allowing them on it in the first place! When the urge to cuddle strikes, sink down to the floor and cuddle with the puppy on his level. Spend time petting, wrestling, and allowing the dog to fall asleep on the floor. Have a blanket that belongs to the puppy nearby, so he may fall asleep with it.

Here's how to keep your dog off the couch:

Imagine the dog running head first into a glass wall. Firmly push the dog off of the couch without any verbal discussion. Then, as the dog sets up to leap or climb onto the couch again, move an open hand (with palm facing out) straight to the dog's face or chest.

The face is your best option, as it leads the dog to the correct conclusion. Meet the dog with your hand as it is in motion to get up on the couch.

Remember; don't say anything while you're doing this. The size of the dog will determine how much strength you will need to stop him.

Now let's assume the dog successfully makes it onto the couch, and will not get off. Grab on to its collar and pull it off the furniture. Keep in mind that when pulling the dog off, your movements must be quicker than the dog's. You should be pulling fast enough to cause the dog to scramble to regain its footing. If this action is done too slowly, the dog will continuously jump up on the couch.

Your puppy's domain is also on the floor. When your puppy attempts to climb onto the couch while you are sitting there, you will need to say "NO!" in a firm and deep tone.

Follow that up with blocking her by the palm of your hand if she tries again. This is not a loving, gentle action. It is quick and firm, and shows your puppy that she will not get past the hand. You need to set a standard at all times where you operate from a position of strength to control any unacceptable behaviour.

Don't ever act out toward your dog, but do keep above them in controlled strength.

How can you know how much force to use when pushing your puppy off the couch? Easy. If your puppy tries to get up onto the couch again, you didn't use enough. If your puppy looks at you oddly and does not attempt to try again, then you have succeeded for that round.

Quite simply, if you let your dog win, then you will lose!

Chapter 5

Hand Friendly

What are the three major body parts people will touch on a dog?

1. Head
2. Hindquarters
3. Side (rib cage)

Hand Friendly Massage

Familiarizing your dog to touch is more important than people realize. Teaching your dog to relax and feel comfortable enough to allow his or her feet and body to be touched or massaged is important, not to mention pleasurable!

Have you ever massaged your jaw or had somebody massage your jaw for you? Try it for the next three to five minutes. Now imagine offering your dog that kind of pleasure. Can you imagine how it would relax them and place them into a happy and contented state of mind?

I watched Rob, a friend of mine, stretch out his Golden Retriever, "Bear" while we stopped for a rest during a mountain biking trip. When we arrived back home, Rob stretched out Bear again and gave him a vigorous rub-down. Rob is religious about this type of care for his dog. I have never seen Bear stiff after vigorous exercise.

Bear's great health at the ripe old age of thirteen is a wonderful testament to the time and loving-care Rob has invested in his dog.

Let's face it, massage does the body good. I strongly suggest that after a romp at the park or a walk or run, that you take time out for a little canine rubdown.

Here's How to Do It

Massaging the Legs and Paws:

Start by stretching out your dog's legs. Place her into a "down" position. Slowly move your hands across the body, massaging slowly and gently. Once the eyes become heavy, stand above your dog's head and pull up slowly on her front legs, gripping the paws. Do this slowly. Now allow her head to tilt back slightly. Massage the front legs, or as I call them, their "arms". Repeat the same procedure on her hind legs.

I don't know many people who don't like their forearms lightly stroked. You can also try this with your dog: stroke up and down the inside of the arm and see how your dog feels. Now try stroking the outside, and see if he likes your touch faster or slower.

Massaging the Face and Jowls:

Mouth massaging has numerous benefits. Massaging your dog's mouth will teach your dog to be kinder and more aware of how much pressure is too much. When your dog touches your hand or finger with their mouth or teeth, say "OUCH" in a high-pitched voice. By doing this, you will communicate to your dog that it hurt. Your dog will then learn to be gentle, and will move their mouth slowly, when either yours or anyone else's hand is in their mouth. Be sure to allow your dog to grant permission to you to massage the inside of the gums and to rub the jowls.

First, pull and tug at the jowls gently. Massage as you would your own face. You will learn which body parts are more sensitive to your dog by what type of reaction you get. If you hear your dog whine, you will know when you have applied more force than necessary. If you do apply too much force, then it is your responsibility to acknowledge your dog's response by immediately releasing and apologizing. Remember how your dog reacted to you and your touch, as this is very important.

Building your dog's confidence in your touch is the goal.

Use a soft voice while massaging your dog, and spend time touching her toes and taking her pulse.

Feel how the ribs move similarly to ours. Find out where the stomach is, and feel how much warmer it is than the spine. Inspect your dog's paws, look at the nails and familiarize yourself with the shoulders. Move the limbs so you understand how they move. What are the limitations for stretching? Check out the ears. Look to see if they need to be cleaned or better yet, clean them just for fun (consult your local veterinarian first, however). Listen to your dog's breathing. Memorize it because it may come in handy if you think that something is obstructing the airflow. Move slowly and pay attention to your dog's needs.

Have fun.

61

Touching every square inch of your dog's body has another benefit, which veterinarians truly appreciate. If you have spent time learning your dog's body and what spots are more sensitive than others, she will be less inclined to feel nervous and bite the vet when she goes for her check-up. Also consider this - What happens if your dog is seriously hurt in an accident? Would you want your dog to accept your help? Just because you are the parent to your dog doesn't mean that he won't lash out at you. His 100% trust that you have built up through massaging and analyzing his body will benefit you both in the long run.

I have a perfect example of how teaching your dog to accept touch can benefit both you and your dog.

Dezdamona's Story

A few years ago, my dog Dez and I were enjoying a day at the beach. We were playing our favourite game, throwing a stick into the water. She would bolt after it, swim to fetch it, and then bring it back for me to throw again. (lots of fun, but pretty ordinary activity for any dog who likes to fetch)

But this particular day, when she jumped off the ledge, she speared herself on a protruding log. Dez immediately cried out in pain.

I heard her scream and I thought, "there is no way that is my dog." The high-pitched shriek didn't sound canine...
It sounded human.

As I looked over the ledge, Dez lay whimpering and twitching in pain. Her eyes spoke even louder than her cry.

I spoke to her in a soft tone, even though I felt the panic growing inside. I slowly felt Dez's body, and she acknowledged the painful areas. This gave me an idea of where I could touch her, and what type of pressure I could apply. In areas that were more sensitive, she would motion with her mouth to my hand, letting me know that it was painful.

A passerby helped me lift Dez out from the debris, and we laid her on the grass to do a quick examination of her injuries.

I asked myself questions as I moved parts of her body to determine what her condition was. Was her flesh opened up? Was any wood stuck in her? Could she move her limbs? What was the degree of movement in them?

I quickly determined that her front legs had approximately half of their full movement, and her hind legs had full movement. I back-stroked the fur on her chest and noticed that an ugly purple discoloration was forming, and that it was expanding rapidly. Within five minutes, she had calmed down and her breathing had slowed. Dez posed no threat to the passerby and easily put her trust in both of us to help her.

I had made a stretcher with my T-shirt and although she cried out in pain with the slightest movement, Dez willingly submitted to having her body lifted onto it. My heart sank as her glazed and darkened eyes pleaded for relief. When Dez was transported to the Animal Hospital, the veterinarian was surprised at the severity of the injury and the amount of internal bleeding that had already occurred. Regardless of the distress and pain that Dez was in, she made no motion to threaten the vet.

Due to the massaging that I had done with Dez, she knew she could trust in the help that I was seeking. She also knew that as long as someone she trusted was there, that no harm would come to her. She was still panicked, but she knew she was safe.

The vet said she had severely bruised her chest cavity and had massive swelling. He told me that Dez was lucky the log was not any smaller in dimension, as it surely would have impaled her.

63

Getting to know your dog's body will benefit both of you. If you have children, it is to everyone's advantage to include them during massage time. Condition your dog to slight pulls to various parts of her body. Find out if she has sensitive areas that are more prone to a yip or yelp, or a physical reaction like turning her head.

Spend a minimum of 15 minutes a day getting to know your dog's body and treating your dog to a massage.

Once your dog is secure with your touch, introduce a minimum of two additional pairs of hands weekly for six months so your dog becomes confident and secure with other people in her space. This is not a threatening situation for your dog, but she may view it as such in the beginning. Stay close and massage your dog alongside the new pair of hands, then slowly remove yours.

Watch her enjoy the massage *(and try not to be jealous!)*.

Chapter 6

Grooming

The Need to Groom

If you watch, you'll notice that dogs groom themselves numerous times every day. Some breeds clean themselves more than others. For instance, the Basenji breed will clean themselves like cats, and personal grooming is at the top of their "To Do" list. Golden Retrievers, on the other hand, will clean themselves throughout the day, but with less perfection.

'

Grooming is an important daily exercise for dogs. As they clean their reproductive organs, ears, paws, mouth, face, eyes, and coat, the dog is helping to keep disease, odour and other health-related issues to a minimum.

After a workout, sit beside your dog and watch how he begins to clean your exposed skin that was perspiring. Instantly, the dog is acting out the responsibility to clean what is not clean. The taste of salt on the skin also draws the dog to clean a surface that tastes good.

Understanding Your Role

Today, the humans in a dog's life are just as important as his pack members were hundreds of years ago.

In a pack, dogs work together as a group, seeking out safety, hunting together, and interacting with one another on a personal level. Part of this interaction is grooming and cleaning one another to keep diseases out of the pack. Grooming may also ensure that pack members bond with one another.

As a member of your dog's pack, your grooming role is very important.

Brushing your dog's coat loosens and removes parasites, insects, and dead fur. Cleaning his ears with a cotton ball or swab keeps debris and mites under control. Brushing the dog's teeth lowers the probability of tooth decay and plaque build-up. Periodically cleaning the sleep away, and checking the eyelids for dirt particles, ensures healthy eyes.

Tools for Grooming

Brushes come in many shapes and sizes. The bristles should be firm on the brush. If the dog's coat is long, then the bristles on the brush should be long in length (1/2-1 inch long).
A long bristle brush works well for breeds like the Boarder Collie, Sheltie or Lasa Apso. With a shorthaired coat, you will need a brush or comb that has short teeth or bristles. A short-tooth horse brush works well for a Beagle, Rottweiler, or Jack Russell.

Nail Clippers are essential for indoor dogs, or dogs who are not actively exercising on all surfaces. I recommend monthly nail trimmings.

Bath Products ultimately come down to a personal preference. The two items you will definitely need are shampoo and conditioner. If you need help in choosing these, find a reputable groomer and ask for their advice. Usually, they will be able to recommend the best products for specific breeds.

Scissors are also a vital tool if your dog has long hair that is prone to knots. In the spring, you may need to cut out large mats that have formed on the dog. A mat is a clump of hair that is being shed, but that cannot escape the dog's body because it has become entangled with new hair. Cutting out matted areas on your dog will help keep your dog cool and a lot more comfortable

Cotton Swabs are great tools to clean out dirt, ear mites, and to dry up any water that may be sitting inside a floppy ear. To soak up water in the ear, you should use a cotton ball and not a cotton swab.

Care for the Coat

Once you have chosen the correct brush for your dog's hair length, then you can begin to care for his coat. When brushing your dog, you will be brushing in four directions: east, west, north, and south.

1) Brush from your dog's head to the tip of its tail.

2) Start in the middle of the spine and brush all the way to its' under belly, doing this on both sides of the dog.

3) Reverse your brush direction, starting at the hindquarters and using short strokes, brush the coat towards the dog's head.

4) Begin on the underbelly and brush upwards to the dog's spine, advancing around to its chest, and then brush the opposite side of the dog.

Take special care on medium to longhaired dogs with floppy ears. With your free hand, hold the ear straight up and gently brush the hair underneath and around the dog's neck and jowls.

The tail should be back-brushed with short strokes and lots of care. The final brush strokes should follow the direction of your dog's coat.

Tips: Take short strokes, be gentle, and don't tear or rip hair out with the brush. Also, brush the dog outside, as it saves on house cleaning !

Care for the Ears

Ear mites are the most common ear problem that dogs encounter. Ear mites are small, black in color, and they multiply quickly.

Cleaning your dog's ears with a cotton swab or cotton ball once a month is a good practice to maintain. If you encounter a mite problem, clean out as many mites as possible with the cotton swab and then treat the ear with a Red Rose tea bag.

Getting Rid of Ear Mites

Here is how to do it:

Moisten the tea bag with lukewarm water. Dab inside the ear and let it sit for a couple of minutes. Roll the tea bag around inside the ear. Repeat this twice a day. Complete the full cleaning practice for three days. After three days, smell the ear. If you cannot smell anything, then monitor and clean ears periodically. If there is still pungent odour after this treatment, take the dog to the veterinary clinic.

Pinna

Ear Canal

Auricular Cartilage

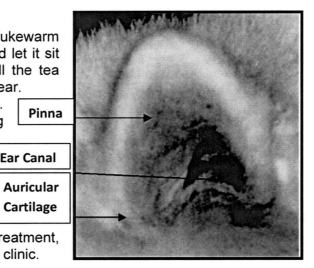

Care for the Feet and Nails

Your dog's paws are vital! They are her only natural mode of transportation.

Unfortunately, many active people do not consider the surfaces their dogs are traveling over when their owner is out exercising. Asphalt, gravel, salt and snow can all take a toll on your dog's feet. Active dogs need to have their pads checked periodically.

The front paws have six pads. The rear paws have five pads. Indoor or housedogs have delicate pads compared to an active dog that frequents the park or is taken for long walks on various surfaces.

The dog's paw pads can peel when he is traveling on a surface that he is not conditioned to, such as hot asphalt, running along the beach on coral, playing on rocky surfaces, or running a great length on pavement. These situations can cause peeling to an unconditioned pad. This is similar to a human trying to walk everywhere in bare feet after they have worn shoes for six months. Just like our feet, a dog's paws can be fragile and be easily damaged.

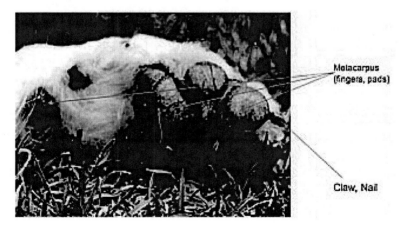

Metacarpus
(fingers, pads)

Claw, Nail

Trimming the toenails is a crucial practice with dogs that do not get out to exercise on various surfaces with different textures. For example, grass is not a durable surface, so it won't

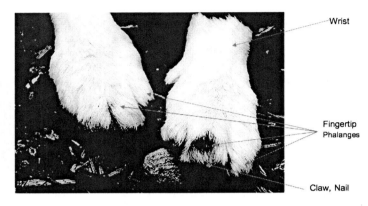

Wrist

Fingertip Phalanges

Claw, Nail

wear down a dog's nails like a sidewalk or rocky trail.

Trimming your dog's nails should be done when your dog is tired following a heavy exercise session or a full day of activity. The "quick" inside the dog's nail carries blood, and this is easy to see on a white or clear nail. White nails are therefore easier to trim with less error, while black nails need to be approached with caution and patience because you cannot see the quick as easily on them.

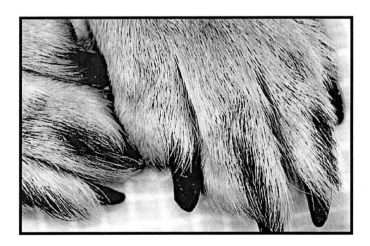

When first approaching your dog to do a nail trimming, massage to the dog's feet while he sleeps, and begin to speak quietly. Massage each foot slowly while stretching the toes. Start with the easiest nail, and trim a small amount off of it (2 mm at a time). Be careful not to clip the nail too short. If you do, your dog will yelp and try to escape. Trust is a major factor here. If you are kind and cause no harm, you will be able to trim your dog's nails without a fuss.

If you accidentally cut the quick, there may be extensive bleeding. Apply a cool cloth around the dog's foot and keep your dog settled in one spot in a "down-stay". Don't let him get up and walk away. The average time for bleeding to stop is twenty minutes. You can find a stopper ointment for nails at local pet stores.

Care for the Teeth

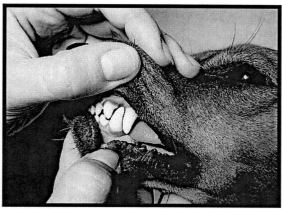

When checking your dog's mouth, it is particularly important that you pay attention to the gum line. This area will tell you if there is a problem and where that problem is.

If you see puss secretions coming from the gum line, you may be dealing with an abscessed tooth and you should seek medical attention immediately. An abscessed tooth can mean the death of your dog if not treated.

Never use human toothpaste to brush your dog's teeth, as it will make your dog very ill. Instead, look for canine toothpaste and brushes from your local pet store.

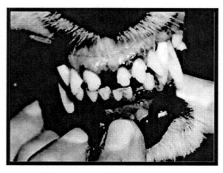

Before you begin brushing your dog's teeth and gums, practice rubbing your index finger in your dog's mouth, feeling each individual tooth. Massage the gums on both the upper and lower jaws. Try to practice this a few times a day for four days before introducing the finger toothbrush.

your finger toothbrush.

After a day, follow up with toothpaste on

Visually get to know the dog's mouth, color of teeth, gums, and tongue. Does your dog's breath smell all the time, or only once in awhile?

71

Some dogs do not show pain, so you need to be able to tell when something changes on their physical body. It is therefore important that you become familiar with your dog when he or she is 100% healthy, so you can tell if something's wrong when they're not.

Care for the Eyes

When it comes to eye care, some breeds need little or no help from anyone but themselves. Unfortunately, there are many breeds around the world that require a helpful hand.

The Pug, in particular requires cleaning or at least monitoring, weekly. Breeds, such as the Cocker Spaniel who have a constant running tear, need to be tended to regularly as well.

With all breeds, clean the eyes with saline solution to rinse debris that was not able to escape voluntarily or from normal canine grooming practices.

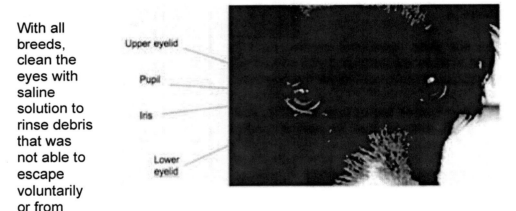

If not attended to, a build-up can form into a crust, making it uncomfortable for the dog and difficult to clean. Cleaning the build-up requires a wet face cloth with lukewarm water. Dampen the crust formation for a few seconds to soften it first, and then gently scrape it away with your fingernail.

Become familiar with each eye; visually making notes of any black dots that appear and monitor any growth. If you see growth in any of these spots, take your dog to your veterinarian or animal eye specialist immediately.

Do not allow your dog to poke his head out of a moving vehicle. Insects, dust particles, seeds, and other debris in the air are potentially damaging to your dog's eyes. An insect that strikes the eye can cause blindness or irreversible damage.

Drying of the eye is another danger that can damage the entire eye over time.

Remember to check your dog's eyes regularly to ensure that you catch potential problems early.

Grooming will depend on your dog and their activities.
So use common sense in keeping your dog clean.

Chapter 7

Establishing Your Alpha Role

"ALPHA" - What does it mean?

Leader? - Pack organizer? …Alpha means Boss!

The role of Alpha carries with it the responsibility for the leadership, safety, and care of the pack.

I believe it is very important to focus on establishing an Alpha relationship with your dog.

If you work on these simple techniques and exercises, you will come to understand the degree of importance associated with the position you hold in the pack and how your Alpha responsibilities need to be played out in everyday activities with your dog. From entering a house, to who eats first, the small details are just as important as the big ones. Piece by piece, in everything you do, you teach your dog the Do's and Don'ts of its world.

75

Through trial and error, and by noticing your dog's different reactions and responses to these exercises, you will define your position as Alpha.

Every now and then, you may have some doubts that your dog still sees you in that top position. That's natural, and your dog will need constant reminding of whose boss.

How do you clarify your new role as Alpha?

There are a number of daily tests that you can use to further the Alpha teaching. A simple "come", for example, may turn into a game of "catch me if you can". You test the dog and the dog tests you. How you win and how you lose will determine what your dog thinks of you and how much respect he or she will have for you. It is important not to lose your head. Being calm, cool, and collected is a definite must when working with your dog!

Who is stronger? It is extremely important to demonstrate (calmly) that you are physically stronger than your puppy/dog, regardless of its' size, age, or breed.

Umbilical Training

Umbilical training is a great way to start establishing your role as Alpha with your puppy or dog.

Um-bil-I-cal (um bil I kel) What a great word! It can mean the difference between life and death for your pet.

Regardless of the size of the dog you work with, this form of training works, resulting in a strong bond between you. Your pet-in- training will learn to trust in you as the Alpha, knowing that you will not bring harm to them.

All of this will be accomplished successfully, without you opening your mouth to tell the dog what to do or where to go.

So, how do we set up for umbilical training?

With the Martingale Collar already on, start with a six- foot leash made with nylon (three quarters of an inch in width is best). Feed the clasp through the handle, forming a large loop. Now fasten the clasp to your dog's collar. Once the leash is attached, step into the loop that you have just created, and pull it up to your waist. This loop should be snug around your waist.

This is hands-free training; so don't touch the leash with your hands.

Begin walking around, turn sharply, and step in front of your dog. Now change direction, moving quickly.

Remember not to touch the leash, as touching and/or guiding the lead to address the dog defeats the whole purpose of the exercise.

Many people also move slower than normal when first starting out in this exercise. The object, however, is to teach your dog to watch you intently. In doing this, he will recognize that you're the Alpha and learn to anticipate your movements. Always use your normal day-to-day pace or faster.

When just starting out, try to do two hours of umbilical training as your minimum daily requirement. This time can be broken up into smaller

77

sessions, if your schedule requires it. Watching television or sitting down for an hour or more with the dog attached to your waist is also classified as training (that should be good news for all the TV addicts out there).

Keep in mind that with the umbilical exercise, the whole point is that you are controlling the dog's movement. YOU make all the choices as to when, where, and how far you are going to move. In Alpha training, you are the Boss, and it is your job to ALWAYS win with your dog!

When the dog challenges you, wanting to pull to the side or backwards, then just continue moving forward until the dog gives in. At this point, you may choose to end training for the day. Just keep in mind to always end on a successful note, when you're in control, not your dog.

It is crucial to include the entire family in the exercises when doing the Umbilical Training with your dog. If just Mom and Dad work with the dog, then it will only learn to follow them and to treat them as Alpha leaders. If the dog believes it ranks above the children in the pack, it may begin to bite and try to physically dominate them. When the entire family is involved however, the dog learns that it needs to listen to and to watch everyone, and that it is the lowest ranking member of the family.

Basic movement with and without the use of umbilical:

Stand up straight and be natural. Move at your normal pace; do not muffle your footsteps. Be consistent and natural, making as few concessions in your movement as possible. The object is to get the dog to make the concessions and give you the right of way.

Test your dog to see if the umbilical training worked. Try it in a dog park or a safe area that is away from a lot of roads and traffic.

- First, ask your dog to sit without using a leash to provoke the action.
- Next, ask your dog to lay down, again without using the leash.

- Now for fun, let your dog off the leash, wait ninety seconds, and then call him.

If he responds immediately, then you have taught your dog well so far. If your dog doesn't respond immediately or at all, then it's not his fault;

It's yours. You need to accept full responsibility. Not many of us like to admit fault, but please understand that you are your dog's teacher.

So, what do you do when you realize that the umbilical training didn't work?

Re-read the how-tos of umbilical training, and repeat the exercise daily until you have established Alpha with your dog.

Keep in mind that you will have to repeat the umbilical training exercises every now and then, even after your dog knows your place as Alpha. It is also a good idea to perform a few days of umbilical training when you pick up your dog from a sitter after a vacation, as your dog may need a "refresher Alpha course" after it has been away from the family.

Many of my students do not take the ongoing aspects of training very seriously; telling me that they are getting too busy, and that they will work on training tomorrow. You are here today, so start working on it NOW, because tomorrow may be too late.

The number one reason dogs are killed when off-leash is not because they are off-leash, but because the owner did not invest the time to train their dog properly in the first place. For some dogs, tomorrow will never come.

If you did the umbilical exercises reliably, but your dog still doesn't see you as the Alpha, then ask yourself:

Did I walk slower than my normal speed?

Just because the dog is attached to your waist doesn't mean that you have an anchor tied to you. Move freely - if your dog moves with you, fabulous. If your dog rebels and challenges you, challenge back (by continuing to move and letting the leash pull him) and make sure you control the ALPHA position. If you don't move and make the dog follow, however, the dog will manipulate you to accommodate him, thus placing you in a lower rank.

Did I hold the leash?

When you try to accommodate your movement to coincide with the dog's movement, you will be reversing the effects of this training method. Please do not shorten the leash between the two of you by holding on to it, because you are cheating your dog and slowing down the learning process. Let go of the leash and proceed with your natural body movements. Allow your dog to learn from you, naturally.

Follow vs. Lead

"I choose to follow. I trust you, and your path will keep me safe. Show me the way and where we are going safely." -Your Dog

I think the responsibility to lead one's dog is more complex than many people think. As a puppy, a dog will gladly follow, as it knows no better. The pup believes you will be its source of entertainment and that you will introduce new smells and experiences to him. When the dog begins to mature, however, its' insecurities and blind trust fade and the pup becomes brave, venturing farther away. Suddenly, you are not being followed, you're being led. How the pup has been raised is a significant factor that affects how you are viewed in the pack when he's an adult.

You need to think about your "lead standard". What is the standard you are setting, and what will you permit or not permit?

Remember, applying the umbilical method teaches a dog to understand that where you go, he/she must follow.

A dog's natural instinct is to follow the Alpha. All eight dogs choose to follow the woman pictured on page 80 without any verbal coaxing. A perfect example of our social creature feeling at home like their ancestors did hundreds of years ago

Remember that teaching your dog that he/she is safe when following you is crucial when training. Safety is the bottom line while working with a dog in any training situation, as all the tiers of learning are based on their trust in you. As with everything else in dog training, there is little or no verbal communication when teaching a dog to follow, as your body language will speak loud and clear.

Hunting dogs, Search and Rescue dogs, Guide dogs, Drug Enforcement dogs, Police dogs, and Herding dogs sometimes look like they are leading when they have a task to perform. These dogs are trained to understand the difference between working and not working. They are all respected in the pack, knowing who is the leader and when they need to behave like a leader. Verbal, sign, and sound commands can be taught to direct these dogs to either follow or lead. These are all characteristics of a well-trained animal.

Adult Dog Umbilical Training

This section applies to the adult dog that has habits to break. The learning process is structured differently than with puppies. When dealing with an adult dog, keep in mind that there has been a social breakdown between you and your dog. We need to reverse this before you can move forward without any conflict. Dogs will become set in their ways. Specifically, you will need to realign their verbal (barking) and physical (pulling) behaviour. You will also need to re-establish and sustain your ALPHA position. It is crucial to remain in control at all times during the restructuring period. Training reassures the dog that he or she is doing fine, but remember to stay focused on your role as the ALPHA while it is going on.

Here's how to get started:

Begin with two hours of umbilical training per day. If you have a partner and/or a family, include them in this daily training time. This will establish your Alpha role, and will help your dog to understand his place within the pack. It should also make the rest of the re-training a lot easier. Remember not to use verbal commands when you are starting the umbilical exercises; your dog will learn far more from your body language. Next, follow the training steps in the book. It may take more patience to undue bad habits, but remember: adult dogs can learn, and can be retrained!

How to Train Hands-Free

After attaching the leash around your waist and to the dog's collar, you are ready to begin. Your dog may get excited; assuming it will be going for a walk outside. Ignore this behaviour, and begin walking around the house with your dog watching you and following.

As you turn a corner, do not touch the lead with your hand and just ignore the leash. Next, go into the kitchen and grab two cans of food out of the cupboard and place one in either hand. The reason I want you to hold on to these cans is to keep your hands preoccupied. This will help you break the habit of touching the leash. As the next few days pass and you continue this exercise, you will graduate to talking on the phone and drinking a glass of water as you walk around (and you thought you couldn't chew gum and walk at the same time!). Next steps: grab the garbage, take it outside, and begin

moving large objects around, all the while having your dog attached to you. Run around trees and change directions or stop on the sidewalk without warning. Keep in mind that pulling is not allowed at any time. If this happens, drop one hand down on the tight leash and give it a sharp correction.

How to Train Non-Verbally

What is the secret behind this lesson? Answer: "Be quiet."
This is so important I'm going to say it again:

Be Quiet!

Do not speak, do not grunt, and do not try to imitate a dog's language….Be Quiet!   Shhhhhhhhhhhh!

Complete silence is the key to your success in this exercise. Let go of your old habits and believe in your puppy or dog.

You have taken the appropriate steps by laying the foundation for your leadership, with your position of ALPHA in place. When you walk away from your dog in the house, does the dog follow? If you said yes, then you're on the right track. Your efforts to train your dog with body language (through umbilical training) should speak for themselves.

If you said "No", then you must return to copious amounts of practice with the umbilical to guide your dog in the right direction. Accidents and setbacks may happen along the way, so be patient. learn from your mistakes and remember to allow your dog to make mistakes too.

Be silent, be trustworthy, and believe in your dog. Give room for them to grow, all the while in silence.

Never Stop Training Your Dog!

Understand, when training dogs under the age of eleven months, that this is a critical time in their lives. Your dog learns the most in this time period; therefore, it is not in yours or your dog's best interest to train him incorrectly.

Most owners who have a puppy often bring training/teaching to a slow trickle or complete halt while the dog is still a puppy or shortly after the age of one year, assuming the dog has learned what needs to be learned and that the dog will retain all that knowledge.

If we humans were only taught until the age of six years, would that be sufficient for the rest of our lives? Of course not! With only six years of training, how would we find a job, pay a mortgage, or drive? Just like humans, dogs need time, effort, and ongoing learning throughout their whole lives.

How to Pin Your Dog:

My rules are: Never quit, never give up, strive for success, and succeed!

Note that this exercise is not "rolling the dog on his back", which can be dangerous.

This exercise is equally as important as the Umbilical Training in establishing your Alpha position. I have all my clients perform this twice a day for a minimum of one week. I recommend you do a minimum of twenty repetitions; however you may need to do more.

Reactions to be aware of during this exercise are grumbling, whining, heavy-breathing, yipping, shrieking, clawing, thrashing, and throwing back the head.

What your dog has gotten with previously will be a factor in how your dog responds to this exercise. If your dog believes that it has some Alpha dominance in your pack, you will have a harder time. In extreme cases, some dogs that were totally household dominant in their families have defecated or urinated during this exercise. **Never stop this exercise until you have won!**

The pinning exercise may take up to 1 hour. Wear long sleeves and if your dog is prone to snapping or biting, prepare him with a properly fitted muzzle.

1. Size the collar so you have one thumb width between the two loops when pulled snug from the top of the neck to below the ears.

2. Remove the leash if it is fastened to the collar.

3. Ask the dog to come with you as you guide the dog to an open space on the floor. Gently holding onto the collar, guide the dog to a non-slippery floor surface. Carpet, Astroturf, and rubber floor are good training surfaces. Good outdoor surfaces would be grass or pavement.

85

4. Sit down on the floor with your legs spread open in the letter V. Position the dog facing you between your legs.

Step 4

5. The dog should be in a sit position, looking at you from about twelve inch's from your chest. Place your right thumb and left thumb under the dog's jawbone. Move your thumbs towards the dog until they are between the collar and the dog's throat. This is very important to have your thumbs in this position. Apply pressure downward on the collar until it becomes taut against the back of the dogs neck. Stop at this point to take a look to see and feel that the dog has no obstruction to his throat.

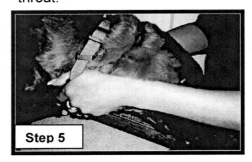

Step 5

6. Apply pressure in a down direction. Apply 3% more strength than the dog is applying. Do not jerk downward suddenly; instead, apply steady pressure.

7. Keep your elbows bent; use only the amount of strength suggested. Hold this position until the dog begins to lie down. Once the dog is down, relax for a moment (five seconds). While performing this procedure, keep in mind that you want the dog to give in, and that this is not forced training with any type of jerking motion.

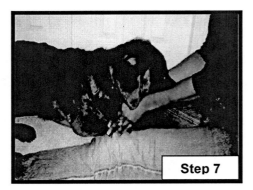

Step 7

8. You have accomplished the first half of a repetition. Now let's finish a full rep: Hold the collar in the same place. As you move your hands up and underneath the dog's jaw, you will need to stabilize it so it is firmly sitting in your hands on the meaty part of the thumb. Once your hands are in position, lift the dog up and place in a sit position.

9. When placing your dog into the "sit", over exaggerate the whole sit movement by moving your dog past the "sit". This will require you to take the dog into an upright position, so the front paws float off the ground by one inch. Do not lift the front paws more than this.

Do a minimum of twenty repetitions and a maximum of thirty for this exercise. Do not speak to your dog while working through the nine steps above. If the dog tries to escape and whimpers or screams, hold on tight to the collar and do not let go. When the dog settles down, continue the exercise. I have found that many dogs begin to act up and fight back between the seventh and ninth repetition; watch for this.

Never reward the dog during this exercise. This includes no verbal praise, patting the dog, or verbal communication.

Food treats are NEVER to be used during ANY training!

"Basic training is over-rated and short-lived. It can be misleading. It may deliver short term results but in most cases it is set up to fail; a money tree for many dog trainers that put the buck before results."

Alpha 101 for Kids

Establishing Your Child as Alpha

Teaching your child to be Alpha with a puppy is easier with a dog that is over 1yr old.

So when should a child begin to work with a puppy? The optimum time is the day you get the puppy. If the puppy is older than five months at the time it arrives in your home, then re- education is necessary, as there will be small habits to break.

Regardless of the puppy's age, however, you immediately need to show him where he stands in his new pack (your family). You need to introduce him to each family member, including other pets, such as a cat or dog. Keep in mind that you and the rest of the human family need to rank above the puppy, but let the animals sort out their own ranking (for the most part).

So, how can we establish our children as Alpha?

First, you need to sort out a schedule so that each family member can help to teach the new puppy. Give each member 30 minutes of umbilical time per day in order to establish his/her higher rank over the dog.

Set a rule that everyone needs to back up the handler who is handling the dog at the time. Keep in mind, however, that you are the "King Pin" Alpha.

If a situation takes place and a family member cannot control it and win, then you must step in and assist the person in need of your help. Regardless of the tactics a puppy or dog will use to avoid new learning, be ready to correct or discipline him.

Children love to help train the new puppy, but make sure your child always finishes any training exercise in a win position.

"Win" is as important as teaching a "Stay". Both can have severe repercussions if you don't work on them and both can have delightful, positive and long-lasting rewards, if your do!

Never let your puppy or dog pull your child; not down a hallway, not down a flight of stairs, not through a doorway. Never. This cannot be allowed to happen. Not only can injury result, but this also communicates that the dog is above him/her in rank. Remember, you as the parent , will need to correct the dog if any pulling takes place, as the child usually is not quick or strong enough to handle the beginning stages of discipline.

To further establish your child's higher rank in the puppy's eyes, make sure they always enter and exit any doorway first, with the puppy following.

89

The children should also eat before the puppy, as well as push dogs off after playing on the floor (if the puppy is on top). Never allow the puppy on or in the child's bed, and teach the children not to let the dog on the furniture.

Finally, teach your child NOT to scream when the puppy chases them, as this encourages a dominant position for the puppy.

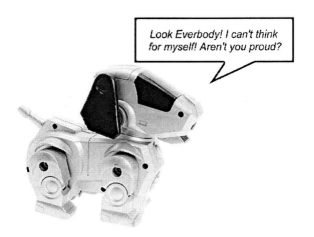

Chapter 8

Umbilical Exercises

Educating your dog to watch you

As I said before, this is one of my favourite words: Um-bil-ical!

Okay let's get started. What do you need? Remember what I said before: one six-foot leash. It can either be leather or nylon, but not chain. That would hurt you!

Call your dog to you, but remember to call only once. If it does not come, go and get the dog, but do not chase after it. If it doesn't come to you, begin running the opposite direction from your dog. When it catches up to you, turn and go the other direction. Turn again when the dog catches you the second time, and continue this exercise until the dog is beside you. Do not speak to your dog to try and encourage him to catch you.

Once your dog is with you, put him on umbilical.

- Now walk into your kitchen and pretend that you have to answer the phone.
- Open and close cupboards.
- Walk to the front door and stop with the door wide open.

All right, now go sit down, grab a pencil, and write down your answers to each of the following questions (there is room in your activity book to follow and track this exercise):

Write your answers to each question:

➢ Who was leading?

➢ Was the leash tight?

➢ When you turned to answer the phone, did you step on your dog's paw?

➢ Did the dog try and walk out the front door?

➢ Did you hold onto the leash?

➢ Did you verbally guide your dog?

➢ Did you repeat yourself?

➢ Did you walk slower than normal?

➢ When you stopped at any point, was the leash relaxed? (without you making adjustments by shuffling closer to him)

And Now Some Clarification

Who was leading?

Hopefully the answer is you. But don't fret if you were walking behind your dog, it just means that he sees you as the insignificant one in the pack. Fortunately, this is very easy to change. Whenever your puppy or dog takes the lead, turn and go in another direction quickly without touching the lead.

AND REMEMBER: DO NOT USE ANY VERBAL COMMUNICATION!

Was the leash tight at all?

If you answered yes, there is nothing to worry about. Just read through the following instructions:

Whenever a puppy or dog pulls forward, to the side, or on occasion, backwards, the dog is making a conscious decision to control your movement, either because it wants to see something or because it simply doesn't want to go where you are going.

To fix this behaviour, you will need to make an immediate correction. As soon as the leash becomes tight (and all the air is being squeezed out of you), you will need to drop your hand onto the leash fast and firm. This quick action should send a message to the furry one, and the dog may or may not respond, depending on whether or not the correction was strong enough. As soon as the leash tightens, make sure to do the hand drop immediately.

When you turned to answer the phone,

did you step on the dog's paw?
I know you hope you didn't, but if you did, good for you!

Your puppy or dog needs to learn that if they do not pay attention to you, they will not know where you're going and they may get hurt. This teaches your dog, "wherever you go, I must follow". If we allow dogs to make their own decisions, they may not choose the safest paths.

A mother does not ignore her pups when they make mistakes while growing up. She will enforce her actions with discipline. When training your pup, the less verbal direction, the better.

Remember: actions speak loud and clear to a puppy or dog!

Educating for Stairs

Stairs can be extremely dangerous for owners when their dogs haven't been taught how to handle them. When working with umbilical training, teach the dog to be beside you or slightly behind you while walking up or down a stairway. As an added benefit, when you are walking on an outdoor trail; the dog will already know where to walk with you. Teaching your dog to stay out from under your feet can be fun!

Implement a game of stepping lightly on the dog's feet. Get the dog to become aware that your feet are capable of tagging or stepping on their paws. This type of training exercise should be done in fun, with a moderate atmosphere of seriousness.

Remember, the key is to get the dog to move away and become aware that they need to stay clear of your feet, unless they want to get their paws scrunched.

Three points to remember about where the dog should be positioned:

1. Your dog needs to follow behind you.

2. Your dog can walk directly beside you, on either your right or left side

3. Your dog should either lag behind you on the stairs, or run ahead and wait at the top or bottom of the stairs (Only use this step once your dog has perfected steps 1 & 2).

Educating for doors and doorways

The mad puppy dash!

More times than not, dogs will see an exit and figure they can leave. The temptation to run to new sights and sounds is strong, and in only one breath, your dog can be in a life or death situation. Read on if you want to curb your dog's "mad dash" out the front door.

If a squirrel catches your dog's eye, how can you train your dog not to bolt onto the road after the moving target? Your dog should not, by any means, be allowed to madly dash out into the danger zone. If there is any doubt in your mind about this, let me ask you: If I blindfolded you and asked you to open the front door and allow your dog to go outside willingly, would you do it? The answer should be no. Dogs need to earn the right to freedom, especially in situations that may harm them.

How do we work with the situation where a dog is excited and wants to go outside? We need to teach him/her "patience". A "sit" or "stay" is imperative to get them calmed down. This sit and stay should be for up to five minutes. Some dogs are born fidgeters, so be patient and consistent in your training and do not give up.

Once they have the "sit" and "stay" down, make your dog sit at all doorways for a minimum of 10 seconds. This will teach your dog to be calm and stop before any open door; thus avoiding rushing out into potential danger.

If you did your umbilical training, and your dog is still trying to bolt out the door, then ask yourself whether or not you held onto the leash. When I ask students to walk the dog using the umbilical method, many people automatically clutch the leash. Habit has taught us to hold on, even though the leash is secure around our waist. We feel compelled to hold on to the lifeline that is attached to our canine companion.

This is not a bad thing, but in this exercise, you need to have confidence that your dog will follow you with enthusiasm. Your furry friend wants to learn to trust you as his guide.

With the leash attached to both of you, it time for you to walk about doing what you do best, ACTING NATURALLY.
For this training to work effectively, simplicity is the key.

First, teach your dog to respect doors and doorways. Stand at a doorway and when the dog proceeds to exit ahead of you, close the door on the dog. Be careful and do not be a brute. You are simply teaching the dog that the door can cause discomfort.

Begin closing the door as the dog is encroaching in the doorway space. Let the door bonk the dog enough to get his attention. After getting bonked by the door, your dog will learn to respect it and to be more cautious by doorways.

Make sure you exit, enter, and pass through all doorways first, with the dog following. If the dog bolts or tries to lead you while on leash, make an abrupt turn and step away quickly, going in the opposite direction from the door you were about to walk through. This will further establish your Alpha role.

Time for a few questions...

Do you verbally guide your dog?

People make one common error over
and over again. It is **REPEATING** their
commands.

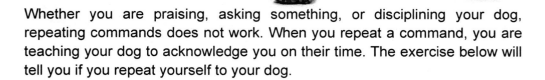

Whether you are praising, asking something, or disciplining your dog, repeating commands does not work. When you repeat a command, you are teaching your dog to acknowledge you on their time. The exercise below will tell you if you repeat yourself to your dog.

Exercise: Ask a friend or family member to log how many times you ask your dog do to something during a set period of time. Keep track of how many times you repeat the same request and how quickly you repeat yourself after the first time, then look at your list and see if there's a pattern.

Training is meant to be fun, so why not make this exercise into a game?

Every time you repeat yourself when addressing the dog, put $1 in a jar (separate from your regular cash), and buy a gift for a friend or your partner from the filled jar at the end of the month. Be honest with yourself.

Now, if money is an issue, I'll bet you will bring this habit of repeating commands to a quick end!

Think for a moment:

When you ask a server for a drink, you don't say it twice or three times in a row (because he or she would probably look at you as if you're a little strange). You ask the server once, and you carry on with other conversation. The same applies to your dog. If you treat your dog as though it is dumb, you will inevitably be responsible for creating that reality.

Here is a trick:

Train your dog in the same manner a mute person would train a dog, without any verbal commands. After all, dogs are not born understanding the English language, or any other form of verbal communication for that matter.

Dogs learn far quicker watching body language than listening to verbal commands.

Remember, the task at hand is to teach your dog to acknowledge you from just your body movements.

Did you repeat yourself?

What a question! Take a moment and replay all of your movements and verbal communication. Repeating one's action, regardless if it is verbal or physical, can send the wrong message to your dog. For instance, if you corrected your dog with the leash, did you repeat the same correction? Did you pull on the leash, and then pull on the leash? If you did, then you just repeated a physical command.

The most common error we make with dogs is repeating, and we don't even realize it until somebody points it out.

Did you walk slower than normal?

Did you find yourself falling into *s l o w* motion? Just because the dog is attached to your waist, that doesn't mean you have an anchor tied to you. Move freely, if your dog moves with you, great!

If your dog rebels, challenge back and make sure you control the **ALPHA** position. When you do this exercise please take control of your movement walk at your normal pace. If you don't do this, your dog will manipulate you into accommodating them - thus, placing you in lower rank.

Chapter 9

On-Lead Basics

> *Psssst! – Hey You!...No not <u>YOU</u>!*
> *I'm talkin' to the dog PAY ATTENTION!*

The exercises you are about to learn will change how you actually communicate with your dog. I will be reminding you often **not to speak** in this exercise, as silence and patience are the best training tools you have.

Your body language speaks MUCH louder than words!

Note: *If your dog is not watching you nearly all of the time, redo Chapter 7 - Establishing Alpha before proceeding with this chapter.*

The dynamics of canine learning have yet to be fully understood with precision and 100% accuracy. I believe the methods I use may be the closest anyone has come to understanding how dogs learn quicker with body language than by any other method of training. By this I mean actual, concrete learning, not methods of persuasion or bribery.

As I mentioned earlier, I do not believe in using food treats as a training aid. Treats mask the actual training purpose, and dogs that are raised on treat-rewarded behaviour are not trained dogs.

If you have a dog that sits for the sole purpose of receiving a treat, are you positive the dog will listen if no treat is offered or given?

The answer is "No"! You cannot be positive that the dog will listen consistently. Once the dog figures out a treat will not be granted, it may stop responding the way you want it to.

Teaching "Sit"

Teaching your dog to sit will be fun, silent, and in the end, rewarding. Here's the equipment you'll need to train your dog to sit: one Martingale Collar, one six-foot leash and one fun, up-beat handler!

Now here's how to teach him to sit:

Put the leash around your waist, using the umbilical technique (refer to page 77) and attach the clasp of the leash to the floating ring on the collar.

Remember, this is non-verbal training and that means NO speaking, no grunting, and no other types of sounds coming from you.

This is repetitious work. You may need to do this dozens or even hundreds of times. Remember that each dog is unique and learns at a different pace, so be patient, do not speak, and stay calm.

Begin walking around with your hands not touching the leash.

Now stop and grab the lead eight to ten inches above the clasp attached to the collar. Pull straight up while holding tight to the lead, until the collar begins to tighten, and the dog begins to sit.

If the dog does not begin to sit, pull the lead up until the collar is tight (and the dog will be forced to make the choice to sit).

If your dog still doesn't sit and begins to flail, pull up on the leash until the front paws float off the ground about two inches.

Wait until your dog begins to move into the sit position, and then relax the lead. Continue moving around and stop. Repeat this exercise until the dog sits on its own as soon as you stop.

At the next training session, begin again. Consistency in this exercise is mandatory, as lots of repetition is your key to success. This exercise can be conducted indoors, but is best done outdoors. Do it at the top of a stairway, the middle, and at the bottom, while crossing roads, and every other place you can dream up.

When you are outside with your dog on umbilical, teach him to sit two feet from the curb every time you cross a road.

101

If your dog does not sit, then place him in a "sit" by lifting up his leash until his body sits. Once your dog is sitting, tell him to "stay", and then you can cross at your convenience. It is critical that you control when you choose to cross, and that the dog understands that a "sit-stay" is imperative before crossing the road or street. This is a skill that could save his life!

Once your dog is sitting 70% of the time when you come to a stop, you can progress to the next step.

The next step in the "sit" command is to remove the leash from your waist, but leave it attached to the dog.

Hold the leash in one hand, while turning around and facing your dog. Now walk backwards with the dog following you. Stop and stand in front of your dog with perfect posture, standing straight up with your feet shoulder width apart. Look at your dog and wait for her to sit. No verbal chit-chat.

Once your dog sits again, back up ten feet with the leash still attached to the collar. Stop and stand directly in front of her, maintaining the ten feet in distance. Your dog should not move around. If she turns her head away, move directly in front of her. Continue this exercise until your dog sits immediately when you turn and face her.

Once you get consistent results, praise your dog with loving, petting, and patting on her head and body.

Hint: Snap your fingers every time your dog successfully sits, and she'll associate the sound with the command "sit". Then, all you have to do is snap your fingers, and your dog will respond by sitting (trust me, this is not only a training tool, it's a great party trick!).

By no means do we want to unravel all your efforts, so giving your dog an edible treat right now is FORBIDDEN.

Continuous "sit" training lasts many months, not just two or three weeks. So try to be patient with your puppy on this one!

Teaching 'Stay"

This is one of my favourites. Clients are always impressed with the end result! After teaching "stay"; they find they have a patient dog that is relaxed and confident.

In this exercise, you will learn to teach your dog to "stay" in the middle of the park with many distractions, and not breaking from that position.

Place your dog in a "sit" or "down" (note the key word: "place)". What I mean by this is: physically move your dog to an area and place the dog into a "sit" or "down" position. Use no verbal commands with this exercise.

Now physically move your dog to a new spot or location. Next, stand in front of your dog, and do not speak. Now allow ten seconds to pass. Praise the dog with a simple pat on the head. Now have the dog move with you to a new spot. Place the dog in a "sit" or "down".

Square off in front of the dog and say nothing. Count to twenty seconds. Repeat the praise, and move to a new position.

You can gradually increase the time that your dog is in a "stay". Once you hit the three-minute point, your next goal can be five minutes. When the time is up after the three minutes, place the dog back in the stay position and say nothing. If the dog breaks again, repeat by placing your dog in a stay. Repeat this until you have your dog stay for the required period of time you've selected. Never quit training until you have a successful stay. Practice the exercise above twice daily until you get to the three-minute stay.

Whenever the dog breaks prematurely, he needs to be physically   placed back at the stay point. Never speak to the dog verbally.

Your body language speaks loud and clear, if you are standing straight up and have a shoulder width stance. Do not cross your arms or drop your shoulders inward.

Once your dog can   stay for three minutes as you stand in front of him, you can move on to the next step.

Here's how:

Repeat the initial steps by placing your dog in a "stay". This time, I want you to step backwards until you are approximately five feet away. Wait thirty seconds. Step back another five feet and wait for another thirty seconds. When one minute has passed, walk back to the dog and praise him by patting him on the head.

Repeat the same exercise ten times at various intervals between ten seconds and sixty seconds. When you have ten successful stays at ten feet, you can begin to increase the distance, working your way up to fifty feet in five-foot increments.

When your dog breaks from the designated stay spot, just place the dog in the exact spot and begin again. Practice this in the house, outside at the park, at a café, outside a store, when picking up a movie, etc.

Teaching "Stop"

Let's review. You are now able to get your dog to "sit", you can get your dog to "stay", and your dog understands that you are Alpha. It respects you, and understands you mean well...Now when you ask your dog to stop, does he obey, or does he slow down or begin to slowly creep?

"Stop" means that your dog needs to stop immediately. If there is imminent danger, or your dog is running too far from you while off-lead, slowing down or creeping doesn't cut it. Dogs need to know how to stop and turn to you for direction. Read on to learn how to teach them this crucial command.

STOP!

This command needs to be definite, crisp, and direct.

This word has saved my own dogs in many situations. I am grateful for the time I have spent educating my dogs to STOP immediately without inching forward. An error can have many consequences, and very few of these consequences are in the best interest of the dog.

"Stop/Start" is the exercise, but the focus is definitely on the word "STOP." What I mean by this is that your voice and body language need to clearly state the urgency of your request or demand.

So here's step one to teach the "stop" command:

Place your dog in a 'sit-stay'. Stand in front of your dog with a distance of two feet between you. Slowly increase the distance to four feet. Next, call your dog to come forward, and as soon as your dog begins moving, firmly and loudly say, "STOP."

As you say "stop", move your hand directly forward at head height of the dog until your hand meets the dog's head as he is moving forward. It's sort of like you banging your head on a low ceiling or cupboard. But this time, your hands are acting as the ceiling, and the dog runs into your hands.

This exercise needs firm quick movements. Keep in mind that when you move forward towards the dog, your body language is confirming and reinforcing the command of "STOP"!

Your dog should sit, because it already knows to sit when it stops!

Square off your hands clearly signalling the "stay" command.

Our goal is to get your dog to halt on a dime with all his paws stopping immediately.

When you are successful from the 4 ft. mark, begin increasing your distance by 1 ft. increments. The rewards with this particular exercise are slow and will only progressively develop with consistency in your training. Watch to see if your dog is becoming frustrated with the training, and if so, take a half-hour break and return to the exercise. Mostly, have fun!

Teaching "Come"

These are some of the most frustrating commands or requests I hear about.

"My dog doesn't listen to me when I call her; she runs around and ignores me."

"My dog doesn't pay any attention to me when he is playing with other dogs."

"I try and leave the park, but my dog makes me chase her around."

"My dog will come back to me, but when he knows we are leaving the park, he takes off on me."

Many stories, but very few win/wins.

Let's see why the dog doesn't listen or come back.

107

Simple - The dog has no respect for the person who is calling him. Alpha has not been established. There may be other reasons as well. For example, your dog may need more exercise. We are going to focus on the most important issue, however, which is the fact that Alpha status has not been established.

The dog looks at you and says "so long sucker, I'm outta here!"

Come on, admit it, you're not the Boss! Nor will all that ranting and raving help you one bit. Shrieking at your dog only diminishes your standing even more. Leave all the theatrics behind and get some control over yourself and then over your dog. Better yet, take a minute some day and watch how funny people look freaking out at the dog that is a 150 ft. away and still ignoring its owner. So what is the cure to this illness?

ESTABLISH ALPHA!

In all seriousness, get a grip so you're not one of those dreaded "out-of-control" dog owners at the dog park. You may need to go back to Chapter 7, and then proceed with Chapter 8 later.

Silence is an important teaching strategy that has been implemented in all of these lessons, and for good reason.

Now, keep in mind the awesome dog owner/trainer you can be, and do not let yourself be dishonoured by your dog at any time.

Like driving, being off-leash is a privilege not a right. There is NO rule stating the dog must be off-leash. All dogs must therefore prove they have earned the right to have that freedom. In the human world, we are not granted a drivers license unless we have first studied, practiced and successfully passed a drivers' test. Only when we pass, are we granted the right to drive and even then we must still abide by the laws, or the right is revoked.

This goes the same for your dog. If the dog does not immediately respond to your "come" command, he should have all of his off-leash rights revoked and should be placed back on his leash.

No Ifs..Ands...or Buts!

Now let's get things started:

Crouch down and open your arms. Verbally and physically praise your dog when it comes to you. Or start running away from your dog so he has to chase you. Leave the leash attached to the dog's collar at all times when doing this exercise.

When your dog consistently comes to you, gradually increase your distance from him.

Here's how to see if your dog deserves the privilege of being off-lead:

Allow him to be free for five seconds, call him back, and crouch down and praise him heavily for coming to you. Now set your dog free again, and call him back after fifteen seconds.

Continue this exercise for a few minutes. Allow the dog to have time to do "dog" things at the park.

Return to the exercise and have fun!

I use the following test to see if my clients have worked on umbilical training:

Walk into the park with the dog on-lead and let go of him after you remove the leash. Walk with the dog, change direction and the dog should turn and follow or catch up with you.
Change direction again, and keep walking until the dog catches up and or passes you, then reverse your direction. If you are leery about setting the dog free, practice this exercise in an enclosed area like a baseball diamond or a tennis court.

This is still non-verbal training up to this point.

When your dog is comfortable doing this exercise, then you can implement a verbal command.

It would look something like this:

Charlie has just come running back to you, so you would say "Good COME Charlie!" Now set Charlie free, begin walking again, and abruptly change your direction. When Charlie once again catches you, you can say, "That was awesome Charlie, you came to me, good COME."

Stress the word you will be implementing in your dog's vocabulary: "COME."

You actually ask Charlie to "come", you do not say "Come Charlie come, come, good boy." …HUGE MISTAKE! But that's okay, because we can learn from that little error before it becomes a permanent habit.

If you ask your dog to come and he hears you, then you have every right to place him in a time out for not obeying. You should remove privileges of independence and unrestricted freedom immediately. Outside, this would mean placing your dog back on his leash.

Teaching "Heel"

Hopefully, the time you've spent implementing this book's training tools has already begun to help you move towards a new and rewarding relationship between you and your dog. We are now going to continue building on the foundation that we've already established with this new tool: the "Heel" command.

After establishing Alpha, incorporating umbilical exercises, and teaching sit/stay, you have taught your dog to observe you well. His new observation skills will come in very handy for learning the heel command.

The following is an exercise that will help your dog understand the difference between walking with you and walking beside you. *(and no, it has nothing to do with that cheesy wedding poem...)*

Attach the lead in the umbilical fashion. Begin walking your dog around and in and out of obstacles, such as trees, poles, parking meters, and anything else you encounter.

Once your dog is paying attention to you and he is walking with you, praise and say "good heel". Whenever your dog heels with you at the corner, on the street, in the park or in the house, confirm verbally what the dog has accomplished in a positive manner. Implement the phrase "Good heel."

Here is an advanced step for the dog enthusiast who is doing great with the previous exercises. You can implement this when your dog is off-leash: The moment your dog catches up to you and starts walking with you (acknowledging your position), then pet the dog on the head and say "good heel." We want to work "heel" in as a positive.

Continue changing your direction and praise the dog, saying "good heel" when he stays by your side.

The goal is to have the dog slowing down, speeding up, and changing directions by your side. The umbilical work you've already been doing will really help to achieve this end goal.

Teaching "Down"

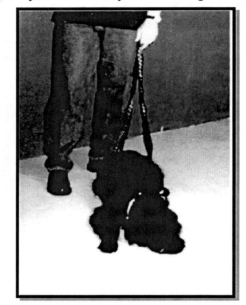

"Relaxation" Remember this word when training your dog to lie down. Teaching your dog this command, which is his natural relaxed physical state, is far easier than trying to teach your dog to stand or to "sit-stay". That's not to say that this won't still take patience! The benefit of teaching your dog the "lie down" command is that it helps to settle them into a calm physical state.

Here's how to teach your dog "lie down":

Sit in front of your dog on some grass or carpet, and attach the leash (hold onto it for a safety measure if doing this exercise outside).

With no verbal communication, place your dog in a sit. Once the dog is in a sit, motion a hand in front of the dog's face and draw the hand downward to the ground.

The hand that is doing nothing can hold onto the leash and draw it downward while applying consistent pressure. If the dog fights or flails, restrict its' movement by pulling steadily down with more pressure. Once the dog is down, sit the dog up and begin again.

As the dog clues into the exercise, you should be applying less effort with the hand that is guiding the lead.

As soon as your dog lies down without any guidance, praise your dog verbally by saying the word "down". It will sound like this: "Good down Tina, good down". Now you can either begin again or take a break from the exercise and come back to it later. Remember to always finish on a strong positive. That means a lot of verbal praise with lots of pats. Like the others, this exercise can be quite time consuming, with many repetitions.

Try to be patient because success will come!

Chapter 10

Patience Training

The 3, 5, 10 Minute "Sit-Stay"

Patience training is about calming your dog (Don't you wish that this could work on children, too?). Many breeds are high strung with boundless energy levels. Sometimes their behaviour is unacceptable and they may be difficult to handle. Reasons for this behaviour include uncontrolled hyperactivity, shirking training or incorrect training methods, misuse of direction, energy, and inconsistent exercise.

I would prefer it if you didn't say "my dog is just a puppy, so he's allowed to be rambunctious!". Making excuses or turning a blind eye is not the way to develop a well-trained dog.

After applying the lessons in Chapters 7, 8 and 9, you will hopefully have gained control over your dog, created a bond, and improved your dog's respect for you. So is patience going to be a problem?

Possibly...

For example, there are some dogs that have problems with separation anxiety. To overcome this particular challenge, we need to target the heart of the issue. The problem obviously stems from the dog's fear of being alone and independent. Then we need to ask why and what triggers this hysteric behaviour? Is the dog allowed on the bed, couch, or people's laps? Does it sit on its owner's lap when in the car? Does the dog lead its owner in and out of doorways? Does the dog eat first, before its owner? When the owner arrives home, does the dog jump up on him/her?
All of these symptoms are pieces to a puzzle.

How to Deal with Separation Anxiety

A dog's separation can trigger many different responses, depending on the dog's personality. The first priority is to ensure you have established some structure.

Please make sure that you have thoroughly read and understand Chapter 7 Establishing Alpha, before proceeding.

Place your dog in a crate if hysteria breaks out when you leave her. When you are home, however, you can play games such as hide and seek in the house.

At the first sign of chirping, yipping, whining or barking, you will verbally interrupt the vocal build up. Interrupt immediately and use a deep tone that is both firm and loud.

When the dog tries again, repeat your verbal command. The third time, physically correct under the jaw or use the leash (attached to the dog's collar) to give a quick snap.

"No noise" will be the phrase to use as your training tool. I am not going to tell you this is a quick fix. I have worked with dogs that have taken up to seven months to educate.

116

Muzzles are also an alternative that you can try using. When introducing a muzzle, keep the dog connected, using the umbilical technique. Do not allow the dog to try to peel off the muzzle. If the dog has a "hissy fit", keep her in motion by walking her around. Muzzles don't hurt dogs, they just bruise their ego.

Now we'll start with the patience training...

Park training for patience is fun. You get a lot of exercise, plus you get to brag about your pet once he shows off his good listening skills in public! These compliments and positive reinforcement can then help keep you motivated to keep up with more training! The ideal time to practice this training is after some playtime or exercise has been granted.

Patience Train Your dog at the Park:

Place your dog in a "sit" beside a tree in the park and ask your dog to "stay". Walk away, and time him to stay for 20 seconds. Praise him for staying and repeat the process, this time for thirty seconds.

When we do this exercise at the beginning of my class, we never have the dog come running up to us after they have accomplished the allotted time. It is better to keep your dog in the "stay" position and for you to go back to your dog. This helps to ensure he doesn't flee, and also works to teach him patience. Your returning also teaches the dog to trust that you will be coming back.

117

The ultimate goal of this exercise is to make distance between you and your dog. As far as possible, so that you are out of the dog's line of vision. Your dog's inability to see you will make the training a little more challenging. If your dog breaks at any time, you need to catch him without saying a word. Return the dog to the original position. Show your hand for "stay" and/or say the word "stay" or "Wait."

Do not turn your back to the dog, as dogs will read a turned back as a sign of weakness. Walk backwards and stay square to the dog. Once you have achieved a three minute "stay", increase the total time to five minutes, and then gradually build it to ten.

Once the dog has mastered the above training exercises (it can stay for ten minutes with you out of sight), test the dog immediately each time you arrive at the park before any play has been granted. Stop at a café for a drink and leave your dog in a "wait" position (tied up) and monitor for any whining or other verbal communication.

If your dog is behaving properly, praise him after a few minutes. Watch for chewing on the lead, shivering, anxiety, or any behaviour that is not normal for your dog. Also monitor for any defensive behaviour and use your voice to interrupt your dog as you approach, not when you get to the dog.

Remember that jumping up should never be tolerated and needs to be corrected immediately. You can tie the lead shorter if you need to, so your dog can't jump up on anything or anyone.

Chapter 11

Street Safety Training

Any off- lead work can lead to injury or death, so be smart and think ahead. Begin your training in a secure area outside. a tennis court, fenced in baseball field or any fenced-in backyard will work. Once you are successful however, do not assume the dog will act the same in another training environment. The rule is: master one training location, and then move onto another as your training progresses.

Teaching Off-Lead "Sit"

You have learned how to get your dog to both listen and watch you. You have educated her on being patient. Now you will expand the trust between you and your dog. If she has earned freedom by obeying your commands, the dog in return can try going off-lead.

However, when an error is made, you need to get back the dog's attention and get to her as soon as possible, as second chances are not in the equation.

Leave the 6-foot lead attached to the dog's collar at all times, with a knot tied at the end so you can access the leash easier if you need to.

Begin walking with your dog, then stop, turn and face her. The dog should sit, and you can emphasize this action by saying the word "sit". When the dog does not sit immediately, place a hand on her head and stroke your hand to the rear of the dog, applying slightly more pressure, as you get closer to the hindquarters.

Begin again and repeat the steps.

Now turn and face her. If she sits immediately, great! Now praise her. This time start walking for thirty feet. - Stop.

Stay exactly where you stopped, and do not face your dog. Praise her if she goes into an automatic "sit". If she did not sit, then stroke the spine, moving from the head to the hindquarters again. Repeat this until you have a consistent, automatic "sit" without touching your dog.

Teaching Off-Lead "Stay"

The off-lead stay is designed to give the dog freedom off lead so she feels relaxed and comfortable with her surroundings and anything that is going on around her.

This is a great lesson if you want the luxury of having your door wide open at the house, without the concern of the dog taking off and going on an

unscheduled field trip! Many dogs I have trained developed a stronger sense of security once they learned the off-lead "stay", which in turn permitted their owners more freedom.

120

Here's how to teach off lead "stay":

Put the collar and leash on your dog and go to the front door. Lay her down in the open doorway. Attach the leash to the doorknob on the inside of the door and tell your dog to "wait" or "stay"

Leave her at the entrance, and watch from a distance to ensure that she is not moving about. If your dog did not move for thirty seconds, praise her.

Now repeat the stay or wait and leave the dog again. Leave for one minute, praise, and then repeat this. Try going outside, and stay there for a couple of minutes. If the dog gets up and tries to walk away from her lying down position, the door will shut and the dog will be restricted by her leash.

Now place your dog (using the non-verbal method) back in the "down stay" position. Walk away again to the same spot where you were standing outside. Wait up to two minutes and praise your dog if she did not break.

At any given time, if the dog breaks and does not remain settled in the stay, simply place her back in that same position. Once you are consistent with the dog staying, then take her leash off and begin the process again, always keeping an eye on her. This is a lengthy process that may require weeks of work, but remember: you will have a great dog in the long run.

The training above works the same in the park. Use a tree when starting this exercise, and get in the habit of tying your dog up to railings, trees, or any other stationary object, for up to twenty minutes. You can either be sitting beside your dog or be at a distance from her.

121

Teaching Off-Lead "Heel"

Go for a walk with the dog on lead, and when the dog is heeling with you, drop the leash, stop, and have the dog sit.

Next, begin moving forward with the dog walking beside you. When she starts to get in front of you, step on the dragging leash with a quick step, and then release the leash. Continue walking, and every time the dog begins to lead, step on the leash. Eventually, she will stay close to you in the correct "heel" position.

Next, when you are walking with the dog, turn around and go in the opposite direction. The dog will follow and catch up to you. Be quick when you are working this exercise. If you move slowly, you will lose the dog's interest. Also, keep this exercise positive. You can turn it into a game with the dog catching up to you. Don't use any verbal commands yet; keep your lips closed.

Now start to change your walking tempo from slow to fast to medium to fast and back to slow every five to twenty steps. Turn in a circle with the dog watching you and staying in the "heel" position. One game to play is tapping the dog's toes with your foot *lightly* to play tag (have the dog on umbilical for this one).

Have Fun!

Teaching Off-Lead "Come"

Your dog now knows "sit", "heel", and "patience", for both on and off-lead. Congratulations on your achievements!

Now let's get that dog of yours to "come" consistently. The exercise with you changing direction while heeling is a key factor to achieving a smooth transition.

Here's How:

Place your dog in a "stay" for one minute, back up twenty steps, say "hustle", and then turn and start running. Yell out the dog's name as you begin running. When the dog catches up to you and passes you, quickly turn around and go in the opposite direction. Your dog will turn and catch up to you again. Turn again and wait until the dog catches up to you. When he does catch up, really praise him!

Repeat this exercise, starting at a five-foot distance and increasing your distance by five feet when the dog has done it three times perfectly. Do not rush in expanding the distance; it's more important to take your time to work towards a win/win.

Never leave training on a negative, always a positive, and remember to give your dog lots of loving after each session.

Off-lead comfort zone is demonstrated with the dog moving at the same speed the owner is.

Human error was the cause of this injury. The dog was hit by a car traveling at a speed of approximately 70 km

Off-Lead Road Crossing

You have learned a number of successful training methods in order to achieve above average obedience from your dog. You now have a smart, educated dog that is a friend, not just a pet.

Factor in everything and anything that you can imagine that could go wrong, and remember that these are real possibilities with off-lead road crossing. You're responsible for your dog's safety, as well as your own, when implementing these lessons in the street safety chapters. Dog ownership is strictly on your shoulders, so weigh out your decisions in street training wisely! I can't stress this enough: use your common sense!

Make sure that you have achieved the training successfully from the previous chapters and that you can get consistent error-free cooperation from your dog, before you move on to this. Off-lead road crossing is serious, but I can guarantee you that it will be very rewarding once you and your dog cross the road without a leash successfully. Your dog by now, should know the command **"STOP"** without creeping or inching forward. He should also know to first sit-stay before crossing every crosswalk with you. If he doesn't know these important training skills yet, do not attempt the off-leash street crossing until he does.

Here's How:

Approach a corner with your dog on-lead, and make sure his attention is on you and only you. No flaky daydreaming allowed!

Stop briefly on the sidewalk, eight feet from the curb, to confirm your dog is only paying attention to you. Now cross the road with lead in hand, and settle your dog on the adjacent sidewalk. Make sure he sits-stays, and then turn around and cross again.

This time, allow the dog to cross with the leash still attached to his collar, but dragging along the ground. Practice this a half dozen times: cross quickly, slowing the walking pace down, reversing direction; all continuously challenging your dog to be alert and to watch you with its' full attention.

125

While I encourage you to give lots of positive praise, I also caution you not to over excite your dog and lose the frame of mind you have been working towards. Undivided attention is crucial for the next step.

Now remove the leash completely. Practice this in a low traffic area with ample visual so you can monitor anything that may be approaching. Think ahead. Ensure that you have ample time to slow down the on-coming traffic, if need be (if your dog decides not to listen to you, strays away from the sidewalk, or decides to do something else).

Work with your dog in close quarters at the beginning, and slowly expand the distance between you and the dog. This can help ensure safe training. Use verbal commands such as "let's go", "okay", "come", and apply the various hand signals you have learned to assist your dog.

Off-Lead "Stop" up to 150 ft

Off-lead "stop" up to one hundred and fifty feet is not all that long; it's half the distance of a football field. Why would anyone want to control a dog at such a distance? One reason is to show control, and to show people how well bonded you are with your dog (or with a working dog). It's a perk of sorts, and it is more along the lines of taking a smart student and giving them an extra lesson in control. Aside from the "showing off" factor, however, there are many real situations the one hundred and fifty plus distance can come in handy for.

Here's an example of when I needed my dogs to stop 150 feet away from me:

Several years ago, I was in a situation where my dogs did not have permission to be on a person's property, but I needed to relay a message to an individual. I knew my dogs had the patience and confidence with me leaving them at such a distance and for such a long period of time, so I was assured they would not break. I asked them to stay, and it gave me the opportunity to deliver my message and still have peace of mind.

Many dogs experience panic when their owners get a long distance from them. So, how do we get our dog to "chill out" for a long distance and the period of time that this requires? The answer is - plenty of practice! Your dog is smart, so let's just practice expanding the distance and lengthening the time associated with this exercise.

In this exercise, your hand signal is to show one or two arms straight above your shoulder beside your head. Big body movements like these help your dog to see the signal at a long distance, or when the light is low, at dusk or dawn. Show both arms and hands like you're demonstrating a touchdown in American football (or you're trying to flag down the ref in Canadian Hockey!).

Whistling is a great sound signal, as well as clapping, or a crisp verbal word. Begin working at a ten-foot distance with your dog, and give a five-minute "sit" or "down stay". Call forward, decrease the time your dog waits to be called, and then increase the distance.

End training on an up-beat note, with positive outcomes. Work up to your dog staying for ten minutes while you are seventy-five feet away. Start fluctuating the time from five to eight, and then up to ten minutes, depending on how much time you have to spend on training that day. Monitor your dog for boredom or fatigue, and quit training if either one is affecting him. We want to develop your dog, not fail him.

Finish off with a twenty second "down-stay", and then praise him to "go play". To break the one hundred foot barrier, just move further away and do the exact same training as you just did with the seventy-five foot exercise.

Off-Lead "Wait"

Your dog should now be capable of a stay for up to ten minutes if you have practiced the Chapter 10 Patience Training with your dog. Patience and off-lead are quite separate, however. Many dogs perceive that the leash means: "No freedom, can't run around," so caution needs to be exercised here. Just because your dog can "chill" on-lead and hang out lounging in the sun while tied to a railing, does not mean that the dog can do the same off-lead.

This is the difference between "stay" and "wait". The first is on-leash with very little movement, and the second is off leash with small movements within a designated space. Remember, off-lead status is a reward, so we need to be careful and strive for success with the off-lead "wait".

Here's How:

Practice tying the dog up in various places and leaving her for short periods of time. Each time that you come back and find that she is settled and hasn't pulled on the leash, praise your dog and keep building on the time that you're away. Start with leaving her for 30 seconds, and gradually increase the time you are away to 30 minutes. This is a longevity exercise that can be worked on at any time.

If the dog did not bark and whine during the exercise, then praise her. If the dog has pulled at the leash, jumped up on people, or become agitated with her surroundings, then calm the dog by petting her for a short period of time. It is important not to dote or baby your dog here, or you will enforce the separation anxiety behavior. A quick pet is better than picking the dog up or comforting the dog with a baby talk tone and over-sheltering her.

Once your dog has mastered the on-lead waiting above, continue the exercises with the leash still attached to the dog's collar, but dragging on the ground. Begin giving him the "wait" command in safer places, like on your back doorstep, and progress to more public areas like the park once he is comfortable. Remember that this exercise will take time, and a great deal of patience.

Use caution, and only progress when your dog is ready.

Chapter 12

Five SUPER COOL Commands
to Teach Your Dog

How to Teach "Rug"

Ahhhh... Sparkling clean tile!...You've just spent 4 hours on your hands and knees, detailing the kitchen floor and are standing back admiring your handiwork...

Suddenly, the four-legged creature you call the "Family Pet" is strolling across the floor, leaving muddy paw prints at every step.

Meanwhile Fido, looking mighty pleased with himself, wags his tail and looks up at you proudly grinning from ear to furry ear. *Sound familiar?*

Is there a way to teach your dog to do the right thing in a case like this?

Yes! Let's teach your dog a new command, and in the end, you can show off to your friends that your dog is polite and respectful of people's homes, regardless if it is a friend's home or yours.

So what are the steps to teach this simple exercise?

First off, do not begin teaching this or any other exercises when you need to have your request met immediately. In other words, don't start trying to teach this lesson when Mimi is waiting at the door with mud-covered paws.

Plan ahead. Teach your dog the "rug" command before the need arises.

Here's how to do it:

Grab your dog and place her on a leash. Walk her to the rug by the door you enter the house from, and place your dog on that one spot.

This is the spot that she will eventually go directly to upon entering from the outside. This spot should not be more than five feet from the doorway.

As you're placing her, tell your dog to "stay on the rug".

Leave her until she is dry, or you are ready for your dog to move. Now you can either clean the floor again, or have a seat, grab a magazine, and smile.

How to Teach "Bed"

Introducing a dog to its new home for the first time is exciting and busy. There are so many new sounds, smells, and sights for your new furry friend to discover. With all of these stimuli, your new puppy also needs to learn a whole list of new rules.

Among these, showing your dog where to sleep is one he will need to learn immediately. Regardless if your dog is sleeping in a crate or on a dog bed, you need to make it clear that the dog has a designated place to sleep.

When introducing the dog to the bed, I always advise clients to take the dog out during the day and to exercise him well. Well enough, so that when play and exercise time is over, the dog will want to have a nap. As you retire him for a nap, tell the dog when he gets onto the bed; "Okay go to bed", and then; "Good dog, this is your bed" "Have a sleep in your new BED". Emphasize the key word bed.

When the dog wakes up, praise him for sleeping on the bed with pats to the body and speaking in a gentle tone.

During the first week, introduce the dog to the bed by leaving him to rest on the bed in a "stay". Then, when it's time for bed, introduce the bed again to the dog. After saying "Okay Max, go to Bed", allow him to get to the bed before you do. When he steps onto the bed, praise him by saying "Good boy, that's your bed, now stay there."

Have fun with this command. Practice this periodically during the middle of the day and in the early evening for about a month. The dog will associate the word Bed with the cushion or crate, and will begin to seek refuge there on his own.

How to Teach "Car or Truck"

Word association with anything you want to teach to your dog is possible up to a point. Car, truck, boat, garage, front, and camper are a few examples. You can teach your dog to go anywhere, if the dog has been educated.

I once met a lady on a farm who sent her dog to go get the cows and put them in the corral. I watched in amazement when, half an hour later, the dog came back with 30 cows and put them into the corral! Then he sat in front of the gate so the cows could not leave!

Taking time to train dogs in a positive environment proves to be the working formula to successfully educate them.

Here's How:

I'm using the car for my example, but you can also teach your dog to go into your truck, your boat, etc.

First, begin walking your dog to the car while telling him: "let's go to the car".

Next, walk six feet away and ask your dog to go to the car, leaving a door open so he has an end point. Allow the dog to enter the car when you are a couple of feet away from the open door.

If he does not go to the car at this point, physically walk him towards the car. When the dog finally jumps into your vehicle, get crazy with praise!

Now try again from ten feet away. Keep trying at the eight to ten foot mark, and when the dog accomplishes it, expand the distance to fifteen feet, then twenty, then twenty five, and so on.

How to Teach "Back"

Sometimes it is not convenient to have your dog in front of you or immediately beside you, and you need her to back up.

To teach a dog to back up, use a firm tone. The reason for this tone is that the "back" command is usually needed for urgent situations. Your tone can change as the dog learns the purpose, but I strongly recommend a firm tone when starting out with this command.

Here's How:

Stand at the front door or gate, say "back", and then open up the door quickly, causing the dog to move back. Do this exercise for four days or until the dog moves back automatically when the door opens.

You will notice that your dog will learn that the door can only go so far, so he will respond by only moving back that much.

Once your dog has learned by the door or gate, you can proceed onto the next step.

Stand at an open door and practice this outside or inside. Now say the word "BACK", and turn and face your dog. Next, "move" the dog backwards by walking straight into it. If you step lightly on the paws, the dog will clear out of your way quicker and acknowledge your command. Practice this numerous times. Your objective is to get the dog to move back about six feet.

Remember, when you succeed at stepping on the paws, be kind and do not crush them. However, if you're too soft in your application, it will be useless. Find the right amount of pressure, and then use it when you really need to get your dog to hop back.

How to Teach "Who's There?"

When you hear a strange sound, "Who's there?" is a great command in order to encourage a dog to bark, growl, pace, or become alert. This is a great way to get your dog to appear like she will protect you (even if she looks like a cotton ball).

Here's How:

Whenever you hear or see something strange, react in a concerned manner and get your dog involved. Never allow him to disappear from your sight, and always practice this with the dog on-lead or in a confined area (such as your home or the inside of a vehicle).

Once you teach your dog to react to strange sounds, he can use his new skills to protect his new pack.

Chapter 13

Corrections

Leash Collar Correction

When you correct with both a leash and a Martingale collar, you need to jerk up the leash with a quick hand movement, and then release it quickly to ensure that you do not keep continuous pressure on the collar.

Here's an easy way to see how much pressure your dog will feel on his neck when you jerk up on the leash: First, slip your dog's collar over your hand, as if it were the neck of a dog. Next, slip the index finger of your opposite hand in the middle ring attached to the working chain. Now give a few pulls on the loop and watch how the collar works.

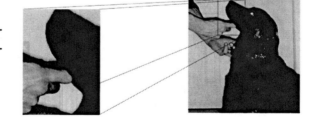

Remember how it felt on your hand when you use this collar to correct your dog.

Under Jaw

Remember "forty-five degrees".

Forty-five degrees is the angle your hand needs to travel upward to strike the dog underneath his jaw. The jaw is made of bone, so you need to know - do *not* strike upward at a ninety-degree angle. Your hand also needs to be tight, clenched, and firm, as a soft hand makes for a pointless correction.

You'll need to move your hand very quickly, because if the dog decides to move, you'll miss (and the dog will get the last laugh).

Across Snout

The beginning point for the strike zone is in the middle of the head between the ears and the eyes. Never strike downward onto the head, eyes, or nose. The nose is composed of cartilage and is very fragile.

Correcting across the face follows the same forty-five degree angle rule that I mentioned earlier.

I like people to understand what this correction feels like, so turn to a friend or spouse, take your hand, and slide it down their face and then run, because they won't like it!

Now, have them do the same thing to you. If you're a fast runner, try doing it faster and slightly firmer.

This is what you will be doing to your dog. The object is to make him feel that you have messed up his cute and furry face. It will be enough to teach the dog using this type of correction.

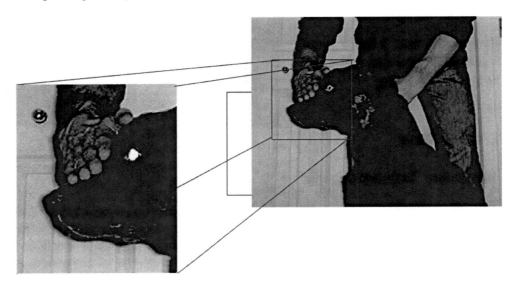

Tone

Tone correcting can be extremely damaging to some breeds. For example, the Boarder Collie can have their spirit broken because of a severe verbal reprimand.

Unfortunately for some of these breeds, the damage is irreparable. You are then left with a dog that is broken on the inside.

So I caution people to never freak out, scream, or holler at your dog.

Generally speaking, men have an easier time than women when it comes to using their tone of voice for correcting.

Each person's tone and vocal range is unique, and each dog will react differently.

Remember, don't yell and scream. Rather, be firm and controlled and use your voice to let them know what they've done wrong.

Verbal

Talking too much while disciplining (and not disciplining) causes many problems. So my rule is, keep your mouth closed and do not address your dog until it is necessary to do so.

Dogs are animals, not people. They don't have conversations the way humans do.

I am sure some of you will dispute what I just wrote. But let's be honest with ourselves, dogs only communicate when they want or need something.

They do not pull up a chair and say, "Hey, how are you doing, did you have a good golf game today? What movie are we watching tonight?"

Dogs don't do that, so don't fantasize that you are having a conversation with your dog.

Hand Drop

The hand drop "correction" is a fake. You fake out your dog by pretending you're going to drop your hand across his face, but you don't. You can use this technique to get your dog's attention…clean and simple.

You would do this anytime your dog is trying to lead or pull you when on the leash.

Jail

No, I don't mean putting your dog behind bars. Jail means something else in dog training terms, but we'll get to that in a minute. This technique may either become a common part of your training repertoire, or one that may only be used periodically. That decision, I will leave to you.

You might want to get comfortable with some tea before you read through the next tale. It's the story of Bart, and how the jail discipline worked to reform his wayward behavior…

Several years ago, I encountered a Beagle that went by the name of Bart, or as his parents would say, "Bartholomew". Like most trained 1 yr old puppies, he was always on the go, always happy, and was rarely a bother. Most days, the happy Bart would join his girlfriend Brandy (a Maltese) and good friend Tucker (an older Beagle) at Dog Day Care.

Bart and Tucker got along quite well in the socially. During field trips, they would venture into the shrubs and do Beagle things, like sniff stuff, pee on everything, and ignore their canine caregiver.

Unfortunately, life's road can often be bumpy….personalities and friendships can change.

One warm summer day, Bart's girlfriend Brandy, a Maltese, decided to seek out a new mate: Tucker. During naptime that afternoon, Brandy decided that Tucker was in need of a girlfriend, and DUMPED Bart like a hot potato.

Tucker certainly didn't mind, and accepted Brandy's attentions…wooing her with his suave maneuvers and Beagle charm. A relationship was born, while another was severed.

Within a matter of an hour or so, Bart went from being the jovial Beagle, to slouching, depressed and somber.

Depression had set in. Bart's heart was completely broken. It's the kind of heartbreak that can't be consoled…and can never be mended.

Poor sad pooch! …You know we've all been there. Bart sat in the corner crying with his back to both his friends and ex-girlfriend.

Two days later, Brandy was over Tucker, and she cast him aside to return to Bart. Unfortunately, the damage had been done, and Bart's heartbreak was irreversible.

Many days had passed since that tragic moment. Bart's personality had been greatly altered. Brandy's betrayal had robbed him of his innocence, in dog terms.

Bart's personality reflected his pain every day that I saw him. The heartbroken Beagle became possessive, and ornery in crowded areas. That part of him that was so willing to learn and explore was gone, and he had become an introvert.

With his altered personality came close calls with his other day care pals. A snarl here and there became more common, and with this behavior, came discipline from his Alpha-leader, Dez (my wise four year old Boarder Collie-Australian Heeler cross). Each time Bart misbehaved, Dez sharply disciplined the Beagle, and sent him over to the jail area.

139

Through much work from Dez, Bart's owners, and I, Bart grew back into a delightful dog. But, he had still been changed emotionally. With Dez's wisdom to guide him, when he did pull a "no, no" in the day care, Bart eventually learned to volunteer on his own to go sit in jail.

So, why the dramatic and long-winded tale?

Well, aside from pure entertainment, I told you Bart's story for two other reasons: to demonstrate that dogs can have real behavior problems and personality changes from having to endure many different types of pain.

Secondly, to show you that aggressive behavior calls for drastic measures, and Jail is a drastic measure. Just like Dez coming down on Bart when he stepped out of line, you need to act immediately when your dog creates a volatile situation or challenges your position.

Using the Jail Technique:

Control and isolate your dog with your hands. Act quickly, and use a verbal tone and body language that clearly communicate that you will not tolerate such behavior.

Place your dog in JAIL and do it quickly! The process above shouldn't take more than thirty seconds tops before you vanish from the dog's sight.

In your house, a jail can be a leash tied to a back door handle. In the day care, jail was in a corner. The floor of the jail was painted white, and the walls had gray bars painted with graffiti that was added by the dogs themselves. I included a metal leash to attach to the dog in need of discipline. Nylon or leather leashes proved to be futile, and they helped to make "break out of jail" into a game that all the dogs enjoyed. Samson, our notorious Basenji, ruled that game!

The metal leash that was attached to the wall was only a couple of feet long. This was so that when the dog was sent to jail, he/she didn't have the option of lying down and getting comfortable. Jail is a method of correction, and when I incarcerate the furry felon, it is to teach them that their behavior is unacceptable.

In jail, the dog is forced to stay in a sitting position. When a dog needs to sit and settle, and their behavior is being controlled, they find out quite quickly that jail is not a good place to be. When the dog is in jail, they are also able to watch their fellow canines (or the members of their family) romp around or settle into a nap, comfortably. This is when it hits home that jail is not the ideal place to be.

Jail time can last from fifteen minutes to up to forty-five minutes, depending on the "crime". When releasing your dog from "lock up", it is not a time for pats on the head or rear-end scratches. When releasing your dog, keep in mind that if you speak in an excited tone, then the dog will feel it is being praised for hanging out in jail. Instead, speak firmly, and do not allow your dog to go outside immediately. Take at least twenty minutes to warm up to him after his release.

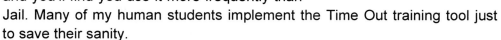

Time Out

Time out is typically used as a means to settle, slow your dog down, or simply get his attention. Time out can be used anywhere, and you'll find you use it more frequently than Jail. Many of my human students implement the Time Out training tool just to save their sanity.

One client in particular had had a horrible day, and her Black Lab was now out of control at the park. She could have allowed her dog to go nuts and to disrupt everybody. She could have freaked out, called, yelled at her dog, and become stressed further. Instead, she chose to place her dog in a Time Out, attached to a tree. She chose the tree as her means to control her out of control dog. While he was attached to the tree, her dog had a temper tantrum. One person that had no clue about dogs criticized her and went off on a tangent about her being cruel to animals.

Luckily for my client, she knew she was not being cruel. In fact, she was preventing her dog from reacting, in his overly excited state, to many different stimuli, which could have led to the dog taking inappropriate actions such as harassing small children, disrupting joggers, and rough-housing too much with the other dogs.

She later explained to me that when she placed her dog in Time Out, he began whining and barking. Those were the two ways her dog expressed his unhappiness. With immediate corrections under the jaw along with a medium and even verbal tone, however, her dog quickly realized the Time Out was for real.

While secured in his Time Out, the dog had no other choice, but to watch other dogs come and go from the park. An hour and ten minutes passed before the dog finally settled down. Then, and only then, did she remove her dog from the tree and walk home with him attached via umbilical.

She chose to maintain control without losing her self-control. Body language, through her physical corrections, proved to be her best form of communicating to her dog. On her way home, her dog respected her and chose not to pull. Traci had not used the umbilical for seventeen months, but she needed to reassert her Alpha position with her dog that day.

Poles, trees, benches, railings, or any object that is fastened down will work for placing your dog in a Time Out.

Be creative; the Time Out can be beside you or fifty feet away.

You can allow people to say hi to your dog while in Time Out, as long as our dog respects the visitor.

You can speak to your dog; just make sure you're using a medium tone.

The amount of time for the Time Out is up to you. Once you are convinced that your dog has acknowledged the situation and has improved his behaviour, by all means, carry on and enjoy your time together.

Chapter 14

The Big "No-No's"

"No Barking"

The voice of your dog is different from any other dog. What you may not know is that his barks can be interpreted in two different ways. Dogs may bark to communicate with others, or they may bark to make noise, just because they want to make noise!

What I am trying to point out is that NOT all barking is bad. There are times when we are grateful that the dog has alerted us to danger or a guest arriving. Regardless of the reason, we need to educate the dog about what we will tolerate and what is acceptable in the home, car, or in any other situation.

Uncontrollable barking is not acceptable behavior. Let's take a look at the barking question that is most commonly asked: "How do I get my dog to stop barking, or at least control it?"

Situation A – Barking During Inside Play

A puppy has just been introduced into the house. While playing, the puppy begins to growl quietly, then loudly, then he yips, and then finally, he barks. Playing? Most likely, but is it acceptable for a dog to bark during playtime while in the house? I would say no.

Here's how to deal with a puppy's playtime barking in the house:

The premise behind this training lesson is that we need to interrupt the mistake so the dog never makes a complete error. When a puppy gets geared up to bark, it is accompanied by a change in attitude. So, what you need to do is say "BOO" really fast and in a loud, high-pitched voice. That will interrupt the puppy from building up his over-zealous attitude. Say the "BOO" as the growl from the puppy gets deeper in tone, or if the tone is coming from his belly. If the puppy actually barks, correct him under the jaw. (refer to page 135) The correction needs to be firm and quick, without any hesitation. Basically, whenever your puppy breaks the barking rule, discipline needs to follow the error. When interrupting an error (like the above example of "BOO"), however, discipline should NOT be implemented.

Situation B – Barking Due to Separation Anxiety

If your dog is barking because of separation anxiety do not get the dog a companion. This will only mask the problem. Separation anxiety is real and very common. I have seen more cases with dogs barking because they miss their owners than dogs barking for any other reason.

Separation anxiety is complex, so let's break it down…

The solution is to give the dog ample exercise, and I don't mean just a casual walk around the block or a quick bathroom break. That is not my definition of "ample". Each breed requires a certain amount of exercise, and it is your responsibility to accommodate your dog's specific needs.

Is your Alpha position clear to the dog? If it isn't, you may have a dog that is challenging your rank, and we will need to trick him and build his security in you as an individual.

Here is an exercise to deal with the separation anxiety barking in the house:

Trick your dog into believing you have left home, but wait quietly on the other side of the door (with the door unlocked) so you can burst back into the house with a loud "HEY, WHAT ARE YOU DOING BARKING?...NO NOISE!"

Follow this "surprise attack" up with a correction to the dog, under the jaw and placing him in a"sit".

Depart from the house again, repeating as often as possible. Make sure to come back often during training, and praise your dog for not barking.

Every time you leave the dog, lengthen the time by a minute or two.

Your primary goal is to lengthen the time your dog is alone. If your dog has not made any noise for fifteen minutes and he usually barks at that time, go back and praise him!

Leave the dog again, and this time, try to go for seventeen minutes; praising him again if he did not make a sound.

Suffering Setbacks:

Oops! The dog barked once at the sixteen-minute mark. As soon as the dog makes that first sound, you need to appear immediately and walk with your shoulders square to the dog (move with purpose). This body language will help you to educate your dog that the bark was not acceptable. Speak in a low, deep voice and say "NO NOISE." You will need to practice this exercise every time your dog makes noise when it shouldn't.

"No Jumping Up"

When does a dog jump up? When they are happy to see you, when they are excited, and when they don't know better. A joy, a pain, what is it?

I have heard so many different stories of dogs jumping up on people. Is it ever a good thing? No, it's <u>always</u> a bad thing.

Let's look at the dog's world: A puppy will jump up on siblings, its' mother, and pretty much any other dog, unless there is a loud strong verbal expression of disapproval. Verbal communication is the key element. In canine language, it is the specific tone that results in the behavior change. The tone that is spoken will direct the puppy to stop jumping up.

If the puppy is unfamiliar with this particular "phrase" in canine language, the dog that was jumped up on will turn to body language. This dog will give a quick and abrupt discipline, accompanied with a deeper growl to address the unacceptable behavior. The quickness in the discipline that is handed down to the subordinate is not always gentle. Most times, when discipline is conducted, it is with a strike from the teeth, but it's not a bite and it doesn't break skin. The action is like a pecking. Another type of canine correction involves pinning the dog to the ground using the jaws as the main "pinning" tool. Again, the dominant dog does not bite the subordinate dog.

What type of corrections do we know that are taught by other trainers and non-trainers?

Some choose to knee the dog in the chest…*No thank you.*

Others yell at the dog…*No, that only empowers the dog to do it again.*

Pull down on the leash…? *Nope, doesn't work.*

Move away from the dog…? *The dog thinks it's a fun game!*

Crouch down and allow the dog to come to you...? *Wishful thinking!*

So, what does work?

How can we teach a puppy or dog not to jump up?

Have you ever knocked your head on a low ceiling, or banged your head on a cupboard door? Did it "smart"?Did the slight bang cause you to duck down the next time you entered that low-ceilinged room, or to be more careful the next time you opened that cupboard door? It most likely did. Well, that learning by association is what I am going to help you to teach to your dog.

At the end of this lesson, your dog will associate jumping up with a very un-cool sensation.

When the dog is in front of you, I want you to watch for when he begins to jump up. When you realize that he's about to jump, quickly place your hand in front of the dog's head, moving the hand in a downward direction and meeting the furry head as he tries to jump up.

Keep your hand firm, so when the dog collides with it, he will feel it and take special notice of the discomfort he has caused himself.

Follow the hand action with this verbal command: "OFF, STAY OFF!" If you have successfully accomplished this, then you will need to follow up with a simple show of the hand in front of the dog's face when he/she approaches and is about to jump again. You can follow up this hand gesture with a firm "No."

"No Digging"

Digging is as common as barking and jumping up. It is a natural reaction and behavior. Did you know that dogs not only dig in the dirt, but they have also been known to dig up carpet, linoleum, hard wood flooring, dog beds, piles of clothing, gardens, and along fence lines? Reported incidences have included couch cushions and an entire owner's bed. Yikes! The majority of digging costs the owner money.

So how do we assess the situation and fix it before it escalates to further damage and even more costs? Age has a strong bearing on the cause of the problem.

I have noticed a strong correlation between the puppy's removal before eight weeks of age and the tendency to dig (see page 15)

Regardless of why the dog digs in the first place, digging behaviors are encouraged because of one major factor: If owners are slow to discipline or interrupt the dog when reacting to the digging, then they encourage the dog to ignore them. I don't advise owners to get around to the discipline on their own time; this will only encourage your dogs to dig more.

Procrastinating with your discipline is a major mistake. As each digging incident occurs, the puppy or dog will see the crime in relation to the punishment.

Here is a common situation to illustrate my point:

An owner notices the garden dug up. By watching the owner's facial expressions, the puppy or dog recognizes that they have been busted. Little or no discipline is taken up with the dog at the time of discovery. However, fifteen or so minutes later (after going to get a fresh glass of lemonade), the owner decides to reprimand the dog for the "redesigning" of her garden.

Now listen, if the dog romped or played in the interim, the owner's reprimand has now been acknowledged as "not a serious incident".

148

Instant discipline is therefore mandatory, if owners want to nip digging in the butt. Allowing the dog to relish in the glory of wrongdoing, promotes a strong desire to repeat the behavior.

So here's the training solution for digging:

When a dog digs or breaks a rule in front of you, react quickly, using quick movements, and discipline him.

When you see him pawing at the dirt, interrupt the behavior with a firm, deep, and loud, "**NO, leave it!**" When your dog moves away from the area in question, give him a toy to distract him, and continue to monitor him for further digging.

Your responsibility as the Teacher and Boss is to actively watch your dog for any type of visible desire to dig. This is especially difficult if you are not home.

What do you do if your dog is digging in the house or yard while you are off the property? Crate your dog.

It is a privilege to have the run of the house or yard. Destruction is not allowed. If the dog engages in destructive behaviors, he needs to have his free space restricted for a while until he earns the privilege to be left out again. Spend the money on a crate instead of replacing property that has fallen victim to your digging dog.

Brad's Tips for stopping the "digging dog":

1. Always address the issue of the destroyed property immediately.

2. Say "No Digging" in a firm and low tone.

3. Physically show the dog the destruction.

4. Place the dog in "jail" for a minimum of twenty minutes.

5. Do not speak to the criminal.

6. When you let the criminal out of jail, say nothing for a minimum of ten minutes.

"No Destructive Chewing"

This lesson is one of my favorites. Challenging? Yes! This one in particular always keeps me on my toes!

All dogs are not chewers however, so you will need to determine for yourself if your dog is or not.

Let's look at what dog's seem to chew the most: shoes, undergarments, toilet paper, garbage, bedding, leather or wood furniture (including prized antiques), moldings, and doors. .....In a nutshell, the dog will chew what he wants to chew (even the nutshell!).

"I want to chew on something, anything!"

Why does your puppy feel this way? Because it's his time to explore and learn about what tastes delicious and smells great in the world!

When a puppy is exploring and teething, pretty much everything and anything is fair game to be gnawed on. A puppy will stop numerous times in the span of an hour to explore, by smelling and tasting. Tasting can be licking a surface or chewing on it.

This is all normal behavior. While the pup is licking, biting, nibbling and gnawing, it is filling it's brain with knowledge (this is not unlike your friend's one year old who gnaws on the arm chair of your couch while you're visiting). This exploratory stage is very important for a puppy's education. The more the puppy explores, the more knowledge the puppy gains to help him spend a lifetime navigating his way through the human world.

When your puppy is in this exploratory mode, you need to accommodate his needs.

Do I mean that you are supposed to hand him your Italian leather shoes and watch him destroy them like a chew toy? NO!

Here's another way to look at it is this: Your puppy will chew anything and everything, anyway, so why not provide him with something appropriate to munch on?

Razor sharp teeth are uncomfortable when teething, and it is your responsibility to have a chew toy available for your puppy at all times.

I don't suggest that you have a house full of chew toys, but you should have at least three (two plus a spare).

The learning process is not always a bed of roses.

151

For example, if a puppy strolls up to a wasp nest that is hidden in the shrubs, he may come away from "nature's classroom" yelping from wasp stings. The painful experience ends in new knowledge, and the puppy will now know to be leery of that shrub.

Mother Nature's rules make a great deal of sense!

To translate these rules into the chewing world, when your puppy or dog starts to chew something of yours, cause a big enough commotion that the puppy will be apprehensive about approaching that object....Now you've won!

Here's how to stop your puppy from destructive chewing:

When you catch your puppy chewing something he's not supposed to like your slipper, say **"Leave it"** in a loud, sharp, and low tone to communicate that you are not happy with what he is doing.

Next, remove the slipper, and replace it with something that the puppy is permitted to chew.

As for that something that he's permitted to chew, flip back to Chapter 2 on Toys.

Chapter 15

Speaking to Your Dog

Causing Reverse or Defeat

When an animal begins to ignore a human command, it is usually a result of "too much, too often." Dogs can develop a lazy reaction when given a command repeatedly, and their response time can lengthen. A dog develops a "who cares" attitude, and stops acknowledging its owner's voice.

It is pointless and detrimental to "over command" or to repeat the few directions that you need to give, over and over and over again. Like a parent

153

who constantly "hounds" their teenager, the dog will just begin to disrespect and ignore his owner when there is too much speaking.

The "ignoring" response is most noticeable in dogs that are highly developed intellectually, but the cause is generally different. In their cases, the dogs that have been intellectually developed begin to get bored if they aren't challenged, especially if their training sessions are always the same. This is because dogs like to acquire knowledge from a broad range of experiences. This need for new experiences becomes second nature. The dog will become disinterested and disengaged when a limited training vocabulary is used ("come," "sit," "stay," and "down."), or when commands are given over and over again.

Deterioration of the dog's listening is the first sign of this personality change. The second sign is body language. In many cases, the condition worsens, leading to a challenge in Alpha, or a devaluation of the owner.

It's called "NAGGING" and it doesn't work.
So, don't do it!

When to Speak to Your Dog

Your voice can compliment, praise, correct, discipline, and signal your dog that it's time to listen. We can use our voice as a tool to communicate to the family dog when she is not within your line of sight or when the dog is not looking at you.

The following sections are five training basics (the "beginnings") that all involve using your voice; these can literally help to save your dog's life in many real situations.

1) The verbal command:

"HUSTLE...RoooccKEEEEY...HUSTLE."

Purpose: To bring the dog back into visual range.

2) The verbal command:
"Hey buddy whatcha doing" or "Rocky come here!"

Purpose: I use this to obtain Rocky's attention so he acknowledges me with a visual glance or look. Now I know the dog is listening and ready to react to my next request or command.

3) The verbal command:
"Good boy, yeah, that's a good boy."

Purpose: To give praise or compliments to the dog for reacting in the manner you expect.

4) The verbal command:
"WHAT ARE YOU DOING?" You know better than to leave like that. You just sit there and DON'T move all right...Man I don't understand why you do that!...Do you want to get hit by a car and not be able to enjoy a long healthy fun life?...or something like that.

Purpose: To use when the dog has done something wrong. To show that the dog's behaviour was unacceptable. Aligning a low tone with

155

a long verbal discipline helps the dog see how badly he screwed up.

5) Verbal command:

(Whistle), "Rocky come here", (whistle)

Purpose: When you need to call the dog over to you to prepare the dog for either a simple request, or an upcoming training session.

Vocal Tone

The human voice can be powerful in dog training, if used correctly. Dogs react differently to different pitches in the human voice. A deeper tone means serious business. A high-pitched voice or scream means, "play" or "ouch", and at times it can also mean serious pain.

In practical terms, if you are praising your dog, speak with a soft, gentle tone. When correcting your dog, deepen your tone to get severity across. Practice the following three tones while saying the words below out loud:

    1) High pitched, happy, medium tone,
    2) Normal voice
    3) Stern, deep tone.

Sit – Stay – Stop – Come – Wait - Hustle up – Okay - Who's there?

Pronouncing Syllables and Consonants

Come – Stay – Okay – Wait - Let's Go – Sit – Stop – Down - Lay Down - No Noise - Hustle Up - Go to Bed - Who's There? - Go See Mom - Go See Dad - Go to the Truck…

It is important to use clarity when pronouncing these words (or the words you come up with). Mumbling a command in a life and death situation is not going to bring your dog to an abrupt stop if needed.

Clarity, clarity and more clarity is therefore the objective when delivering these commands.

Spend some time practicing the command words above in each of their contextual training situations.

Sound Signals

Basically, when it comes to sound signals, what you decide to use will come down to what you are comfortable doing in order to make different sounds. Clapping, whistling, yelling, or imitating a birdcall, are all different ways we can communicate to our dogs when we are out together. So, you may as well get creative!

Here are some ideas:

1. Clap
2. Shrill
3. Yahoo Whistle
4. Clicking
5. Finger Snap

157

It is not necessary to stick only to conventional sounds or noises when training your dog.

Sometimes the more unique the sound, the more likely only your dog will come when you use it.

For example, a friend of mine used a unique whistle that sounded like the start of a song, to call her Norwegian Elkhound. Her dog knew the whistle was hers, and she would always come when anyone from the family whistled that tune.

Chapter 16

Understanding Canine Socialization

The most wonderful word in the dog universe is "socialization."

A Blue Heeler on the farm that encounters cows, horses, and chickens finds enjoyment working with these animals.

The Labrador Retriever that is out with Mom or Dad and a few hunting friends finds excitement in capturing the water fowl that needs to be retrieved.

A Guide Dog that is helping its Companion complete the tasks of daily living, finds the work rewarding.

And the family dog that kept an eye on the house all day feels confident he can ward off any bad guys that may come his way.

These are all wonderful and rewarding tasks that our dogs do willingly and selflessly for their humans. So what are we going to give back to our dogs?

Taking your dog out to visit other dogs is great for building self-esteem.

Dogs learn from other dogs. They learn play etiquette, they learn how to greet fellow canines, they learn right from wrong and the "rules" of doggy behaviour.

If you observe your dog while off-leash, romping around - doing dog things with other dogs, you'll see them learning right in front of you!

Owners that deter their dogs from becoming excited with other dogs are limiting their dog's socialization skills. These skills are needed for them to cope with various situations they will encounter in their lifetime.

It might be a social meeting or just a simple dog pile; the point is to allow your dogs to play like dogs!

Here's how the social network functioned in my Doggie Day Care.

First, we would screen all dogs (puppies didn't need to be interviewed) before they were admitted into the common area. During the interview process, the dogs had a mouth test, obedience test, and met with Dez to see what she would say about the newcomer. Depending on her reactions, I would make my assessment and finally make a decision about whether they could join the gang inside.

The majority of dogs had no problem and quickly found the Day Care to be their home away from home, interacting and greeting all that came to say Hello. Other dogs would wait until the excitement settled, and then they would make their way over to introduce themselves.

Many people believe that two dogs making contact is the first step in their greeting process. In actuality, by the time they first greet each other (snout to bum), there has already been much discussion, and many decisions have been made.

Dogs have various methods of communicating. If you watch two dogs say hello from a distance, or better yet, observe how a group of dogs greet one another, you will immediately notice that the tail plays a significant role in communicating a dog's mood.

Tail Positioning

A tail, down and tucked underneath the belly, means the dog is insecure, nervous, and submissive.

A tail extended straight out and slightly moving, means the dog is cautious and not completely confident.

A tail upright and swaying (more so at the upper half), means the dog is confident. A stranger could approach to say "Hello", with minimal concern of a threat.

161

A tail upright and swaying back and forth, means the dog is excited and anxious to socialize; indicating that he is non-threatening to you.

A tail upright, wagging, and then standing straight up and holding a still position, means that the dog is friendly; inviting the stranger to say hello first and control the greeting with no threat of aggressive actions.

Two tails, upright wagging at the same time, means that there is mutual agreement to say hello and that they see each other as equals.

A tail, extended between two/thirds and three/quarters up with no movement at a solid stop, means there is tension and the dog is on guard. In this case, the dog is evaluating the situation for a range of possibilities, from a challenge to an invitation to play. This behaviour is quite dominant in Alpha personalities or dogs that find enjoyment in challenges.

The higher the tail, the more confident the dog is, but this does not necessarily mean that he is making a statement that he is Alpha.

The lower the tail, the lower the rank; showing submission.

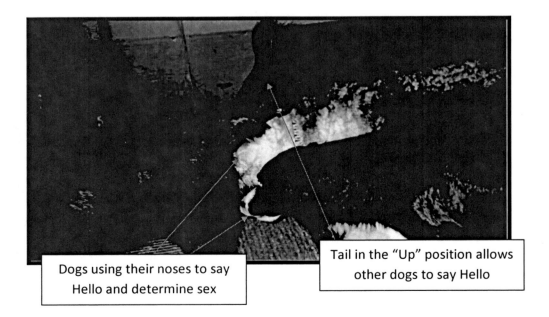

Dogs using their noses to say Hello and determine sex

Tail in the "Up" position allows other dogs to say Hello

Can we as Owners be confident that the tail is telling us everything? Yes, but it is only effective to a certain degree. Understandably, many of you who have dogs with docked tails will find it harder to observe and evaluate your dog's tail positioning.

When two canines are beginning a greeting, what other body language are the dogs using before they come nose to bum?

Here are some other "words" that the dogs are communicating through their body language:

Have you ever noticed that when your dog says hello, his neck is not extended to its fullest?

Have you been out walking with your dog, when suddenly he stops in his tracks, his shoulders become rigid, and his eyes become focused on the approaching dog?

His chest may be puffed up or simply be lengthened by the height of the head being held high. His shoulder positioning may also become stacked with tension or the shoulders may become stiff.

The hair on a dog's back can also communicate critical information. This is usually your first indication of how your dog is feeling.

Upright hackles may tell you that your dog is on guard and that he will react first if the visiting dog says something that your dog does not agree with.

The feet also tell us much about our dog's disposition. While in the park, have you seen a dog that's strutting or prancing on his tiptoes with his tail straight up? This behaviour means that the dog is trying to pick a fight, and you should leave the area immediately.

A dog that has been confined to a yard and not socialized with other canines is unlikely to enjoy playing with other dogs. Learning about play is often difficult for these dogs, but interacting with a socially compatible dog that is similar in temperament makes it easier. It may take a while for the inexperienced dog to learn and trust, but it can happen.

I have seen many people snatch up their dog from the ground as soon as they see another dog in the distance. When the two groups meet one another, quite often the dog that has all four paws on the ground will jump up at the small dog that is clutched in the human vice grip.

My ear is always filled with excuse after excuse why a client's dog snaps or barks or tries to climb back into their arms for security. I have probably heard every possible excuse to justify picking up the dog.

Why do they need to do this? I'm not quite sure. For those of you out there that have made it a habit to treat your dog in this manner, you are the ones that have done wrong.

Let your dog stay on the ground so the two dogs can say hello instead of encouraging the visiting dog to jump up.

Allow your dog to learn how to socialize.

Don't teach him that all other dogs are a threat.

Body Language

If you truly want to be a part of your dog's life and to be the guardian over their safety, then you need to take time to become educated in their canine language.

The language I am referring to can only be studied from watching their bodies, not their voices. Knowing your dog's body language is important in understanding your dog.

When dogs extend their necks, it means that they are lashing out in defense. Watch, as two dogs view one another from any kind of distance, and you will notice a definite posture in how the dogs' neck holds its head.

166

Obviously, a greeting or the threat of an attack is quite minimal at a couple hundred feet. When another dog enters your dog's comfort zone however, another change will take place in the posture of the neck.

When the neck and head are held high, the dog is confident about the greeting and will invite the visitor to say hello.

If the neck is dropped into the shoulders slightly, you will notice a relaxed body during the greeting.

To illustrate how dog's teach each other, I would like to use Max as an example of an Enforcer, as he would not tolerate any dog being insubordinate to either a human or canine.

When Max took it upon himself to correct or discipline another dog at my Dog Day Care, he did it with great skill and was precise in his actions. He only applied enough power to ward off any retaliation. He was very aware of his ability to break skin and physically damage his insubordinate friend.

If there was retaliation from the dog he was correcting, then before he proceeded, Max looked both at the other dog and myself. By looking at both of us, Max was seeking permission to strike again.

"The Enforcer" then made an obvious motion with his body. His neck sunk further into his shoulders, enabling Max to strike the other dog with more power. His head then extended in a quick strike with his jaws; not breaking skin, but reminding the other dog that he had crossed the line.

I have seen this action many times with other dogs as well. The neck will be moderately compressed into the shoulders and then, when they need to strike, the neck compresses and extends in the blink of an eye. I imagine the purpose for compressing the neck is to protect the throat. When a situation is becoming volatile, they then compress their neck further for protection, and strike harder to end the confrontation.

Sometimes, a dog will place its neck and head over top of another dog's shoulder. This is the dog's immediate call to say, "I am Alpha."

One of two things can then happen. The dog that is on the underside may say, "that is fine"; and spin in a 180-degree turn to say, "we can play, but you can't dominate me". This is a very common reaction. The other option is that the subordinate will flee.

A dog demonstrating its intention to use power and to "rule the roost" would have gotten nowhere with my dogs, Dez or Max.

Dez was never impressed with arrogant attitudes, and she would simply dismiss any bad behaviour quietly.

On the other hand, if she was challenged, she would gently warn the other dog to stay away. If the pursuing dog persisted, Dez was quick to react by first showing all of her forty-two teeth.

Max would also come to enforce Dez's actions, and the situation would quickly be diffused by one strike from Max towards the subordinate.

I didn't reprimand Max for stepping-in to assist his older sister. I did talk to him immediately afterward, telling him he did a good job and that it was time to relax.

His next move was always to follow up on behalf of Dez's well being. He sought a pat on the head, and it was all soon forgotten.

Sometimes, a fury of action can unfold when two Alpha dogs come into contact.

Usually a stubborn Alpha, who feels compelled to prove he or she is ruler of the park, instigates this.

This is done by first exerting pressure down on the other dog's shoulders, and then lashing out to cause emotional or physical harm.

If another dog is stalking your dog, leave the park area and go elsewhere, or ask the owner to detain their dog for a short while.

Unfortunately, owners who have out of-control dogs are often uneducated in how to discourage this type of behaviour.

Here are things to watch for:

The shorter the other dog's neck becomes, the less time you will have before a bad situation will develop. You will need to get your dog out of the area immediately.

A long, relaxed neck means a mutual understanding between dogs, so you can relax and enjoy your time while your dog plays with his new friend.

Dogs can move far faster than what the human eye is capable of following.

Get to know your dog, and try to safeguard him from unpleasant situations.

Accidents and incidents happen all the time. Some dogs don't like each other for their own reasons. Respect the choice they make in whom they choose to play with, or to whom they communicate "Hello" or "Stay away from me, I DON'T LIKE YOU!"

Parks can be great learning laboratories for observing canine behavior, as long as we have the knowledge to go along with our observations.

We need dogs of different breeds and we need those dogs to act as dogs do naturally. This may sound strange, but with humans interrupting dogs' play with commands or even with their stares, dogs' experiences don't always occur as they otherwise would.

Dogs don't often get a chance to be dogs. This leads to frustration, and an unhappy dog will act out discontentment through inappropriate behavior.

We have so much to learn from our own dog, in his/her likes and dislikes, including which dogs and what breeds he/she does not get along with. We can learn these important things through simply letting them play and be dogs.

Chapter 17

Doggy Etiquette

Park Etiquette

Even if your dog is a well-behaved dog, never underestimate the possibility the possibility that he could become aggressive if the situation arises.

My dogs Dez and Max have both been trained off-leash. To their credit, they have worked in commercials, film and magazine ads. Regardless of their ability to perform there is always the possibility that an altercation can unfold between dogs, especially if one dog suddenly feels that socializing means being a bully.

I'd like to share a story with you:

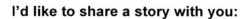

At one dog park that I use to visit, I frequently ran into a particular group of dog owners and their dogs. This group of people referred to themselves as the "Hump" people. They met promptly at five p.m. every weeknight and eight a.m. on weekends.

Let's say that their reputation preceded them.

One evening, Dez and I went for a walk to watch how these people and their dogs socialized. As we approached, I heard a great deal of noise and the odd yelp from various dogs in the socializing group. Dez appeared uninterested in approaching them, so I took that as a sign to be cautious.

I introduced myself to the "Hump" group, and quickly felt out of place. Out of the blue, a Doberman scooted up beside me with a tennis ball in its mouth. The owner quickly piped up and said, "I dare you to take the ball out of her mouth." I thought that was an odd challenge. It was clear from the tone of his voice, that he felt confident that I would fail, and that he and his Hump-friends would get a good laugh.

When I attempted to "ask" the dog for the ball, the Doberman flicked her head and then bolted after a few of the romping dogs.

After a short playtime, she returned and once again stood beside me. This time, I held onto her collar and pulled her up until her paws were floating an inch above the wet grass. Within twenty seconds, one tennis ball popped out, then a second, and then a third!

As I lowered the Doberman's paws to the ground, the owner began berating me for using "brutal force" on his dog and causing it "harm". I tried to explain that what I had done was in no way harmful to his dog, but our attention was quickly diverted. His dog was engaged in an aggressive  confrontation with two other dogs. We could see that one dog was sore from a hefty nip to the hind end.

Dogs learn animosity when the owner has a tough guy attitude and expresses that type of behaviour in training the dog. There is a high risk that the dog will not grow to be a fun play companion, but an aggressive and unfriendly dog. Shockingly, I was amazed at how the other owners kept track of whose dog was up for inflicting pain to another canine. I was sickened to find human beings that encouraged this type of socialization.

Park Etiquette Rules.

Never allow your dog to invite himself to someone else's picnic.

Do not encourage your dog to chase skateboarders, joggers, inline skaters, cyclists, people out on a stroll, runaway toddlers, or cars.

The most important thing to remember is never allow your dog to approach a small child or infant that is screaming or crying. Your dog is a pack animal, and when a fellow member of a pack is wounded (the baby crying), an instinct is triggered in them and they may attack the wounded pack member. The dog's instinct here is to help end the pain and misery of the wounded animal.

If a negative incident does begin to arise, grab your dog immediately and place it into a "stay", or exit the park with your dog on-lead.

Most importantly, it is in the best interest of both your dog and yourself, to remain proactive, and aware of who and what is going on around you. Simply put, steer clear of these situations. Period

Also note that many people are frightened of dogs. They may have been bitten in the past, there may be religious and cultural differences to consider or they may just not be comfortable around dogs.

173

Make it a habit to say "good morning" or "good afternoon" to everyone that your dog comes into contact with. Establish eye contact as you do this, reading his or her facial expression. You will be able to determine if your dog is acceptable or bothersome to this person.

Quickly try to create a social atmosphere, by letting the person know that your dog is super- friendly and likes pats on the bum (or whatever else he likes).

Unfortunately, there will always be someone out there that will criticize what you do.

Even if you are picking up after your dog, even if and they are on-leash – or even if your dog is on its best behaviour and not bothering a soul. There will always be ornery and hateful people on a mission to be bitter, and they all seem to go to the park. Remember that as a dog owner, you will face some uncalled for remarks. Arguing is futile. Try to be cheery, and enjoy your day without letting the small-mindedness affect you.

Remember to pick up after your dog.

Control your dog's social behaviour. Do not allow nipping in play, but do allow some barking. Barking is a form of expression and communication, and does not mean a volatile situation is about to explode. If it is getting out of control, however, then definitely put a stop to it.

Allow your dog to say hello off-leash, or if you are uncomfortable with her off-leash, then let it drop to the ground and step on the handle, but allow your dog to have freedom in movement so she does not feel restricted or confined. Most dogfights happen when either one dog is on-leash and the other is free or when both dogs are on-lead. Quite simply, restricting their movement adds fuel to the fire. Dogs need their freedom when saying hello.

Imagine; if I were to hold you back from greeting your neighbours, would you become tense and struggle to escape my grip?

Of course you would! So remember, don't restrict your dog's movement when he is socializing with other dogs.

Play Etiquette

A gentle, pleasant manner is what play etiquette is all about.

No bullies and no jerks. Just some good clean fun.

Here's more to help you to navigate through the park with your pet:

If a dog is mounting your dog, or if it's your dog that is doing the mounting, one of two things is happening: Either the dog doing the mounting is trying to dominate, or he is masturbating. Regardless if a dog has been spayed or neutered, they still like to masturbate and at times will also have a discharge.

This behaviour has caused dogfights, especially if the dog is persistent. If you see this starting, break it up, place the dog on-lead, and leave the area.

Uncontrollable barking is a terrible noise and is very irritating to some dogs. A mouthy, loud dog can provoke an outbreak of aggression. If you notice either your dog or another start to get too yappy, place your dog back on-lead and remove him from the area.

Nipping other dogs in play is also not acceptable. If you notice nipping during play, remove your dog from his play pals, firmly correct him, and place him in a time out for a minimum of ten minutes.

Here are some examples of appropriate 'Play Etiquette':

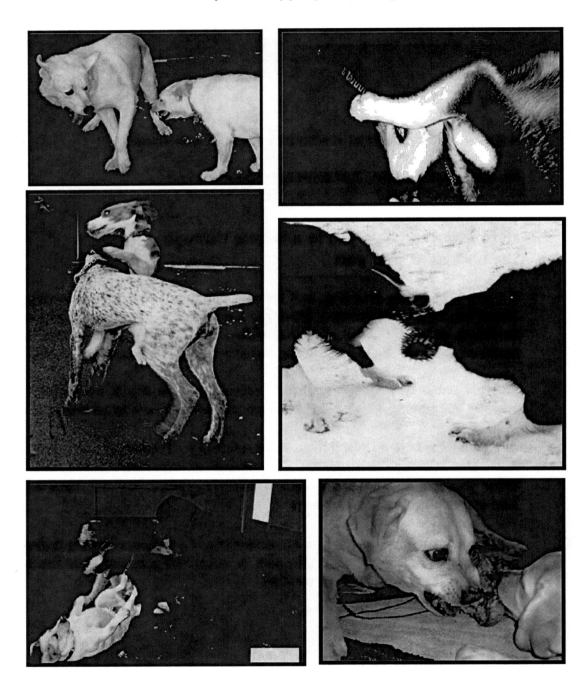

Chapter 18

Breaking up a Dogfight

What You Should Do

The decision to step into a dogfight is open to many variables and this makes it a very dicey proposition.

First, you need to consider some important factors:

- What are the breeds of the dogs that are fighting?
- What are the sizes of the dogs?
- How long the fight has gone on?
- Who is the aggressor?
- What is the ground is like; is it slippery or hard?
- Is there a leash on one/both of the dogs?
- Is one dog ten to fifteen times bigger than the other dog?
- What size are you in relation to the dogs that are fighting?
- How strong are you?
- What kind of experience do you have with this type of volatile situation?

You need to evaluate if you want to get involved, and most importantly, if you can do so safely. I suggest that if you have no experience, stay out. You can always use your cell phone to call for help.

If, after you have assessed the situation, you feel confident about getting involved, and all the variables seem safe, then read the following sections.

When a fight breaks out, the first thing you do is:

Let out the loudest and deepest yell you can. Aim it directly at the middle of the fight and keep your body square to the two dogs.

If you are behind a dog that is fighting, grab the collar behind his neck and pull the dog back as fast as you can, yelling in a deep, deep voice at the other dog and staying square to him.

If a dog is shaking or biting another dog, and you need to "pop off" the jaws, then kick the dog hard in the lower rib cage.

What You Should NOT Do

I have witnessed and broken up many dogfights over the years. One common reaction I see from people attempting to break up a fight is to scream at the top of their lungs.

First, screaming is the opposite of what you should do. You need to use a controlled tone when trying to stop dogs in an aggressive confrontation.

178

During a fight, a scream also represents pain to the dogs, not control or any type of dominance. So if you are going to scream, don't bother!

Secondly, I have seen many people get bitten accidentally when attempting to break up a fight.

One of the dogs in the confrontation usually ends up biting someone's hand. Not because the hand is any kind of threat, but because the person who owns the hand is shoving it into the middle of the fight. Why would any sane person want to do that? This is the question of the decade. I don't know one person who would stick their hand into a blender when the blender is on.

So never challenge a dog's mouth, you will lose.!

Another crazy antic would be to grab a dog's jaw and pull it open. Only if my hands are made of titanium. It's another not-so-bright idea!

Dogs move their mouths and bodies much faster than we can move any part of our bodies. The human hand will always lose.

I have heard people suggest that you can break up the fight by running into the middle of it. Not smart. You may as well run between two dueling swordsmen.

No! That would not be a wise idea either..

About the Author

Brad Pattison

Brad Pattison has been professionally remedying dog behavior for over 15 years. He uses revolutionary techniques derived from his studies of domesticated dogs, wolves and coyotes.

Brad's unique methods involve communicating with dogs in a way they understand – through body language.

Brad founded the first Dog Day Care Centre in

Vancouver British Columbia Canada, creating the concept that is now used around the world. He created the first Street Safety training program, and runs courses that teach other dog educators his skills.

Brad has appeared on CBC's *Venture,* Lifestyle Network's *Gentle Doctor*, PBS' *Sesame Street.*

Brad was the host of Yuppy Puppy, his own radio show and is a frequent guest on radio stations across the country. He has appeared in newspapers and magazines such as *Dog World, Wall Street Journal* and *USA Today.*

Summary

Thank you for taking the time to read this book. I hope that you have found it helpful in better understanding your dog and your relationship with him.

 I also hope that you have started to apply the lessons, and that you have seen results!

One of the challenges in writing a book about dog training is trying to translate what I do and what I have learned from experience into information that I can communicate to you as the reader.

I would like to hear about your experiences in applying these lessons. I can be contacted online at my website, www.bradpattison.com

Wishing you and your dog the best of friendships and a life-long bond.

Sincerely,

Brad Pattison
Brad, Dez & Max

www.bradpattison.com

Hustle Up™ to a New Career!

The Hustle Up School of Dog Training™ does not use conventional methods that "normal" dog owners or trainers use. But who wants to settle for just a "normal" dog? Our Certified Educational Trainers don't use treat training, prong collars or any other methods that "mask" bad behavior. At the Hustle Up School you will learn to use Brad Pattison's unique training system, based on canine behavior and psychology.

As Brad has proven, over and over again, his methods really work!

The goal for 2009 and beyond, is to make the Hustle Up School of Dog Training the "gold standard" in dog training and Brad Pattison's method the new "norm"!

This program consists of:

o A complete course on how to successfully train dogs using Brad's unique and effective techniques.

o Previously unpublished materials.

o Advanced lessons that will teach you how to build an extraordinary relationship with your dog based on true respect. You will experience a whole new world of dog ownership, believing in your dog as a true friend and knowing, in dog-terms, what that actually means.

For more information about the Hustle Up School of Dog Training™ and to start your rewarding career as a Certified Educational Trainer visit: www.bradpattison.com

183

Join a Fitness Revolution!

Many dog owners want to exercise, but where to find the time? When life gets busy, scheduling time to workout can become a challenge.

So what do you do when the dogs need a walk and you need to be at the gym?

Combine the two and you have **6 Legs to Fitness**, a dynamic and innovative fitness experience!

This unique exercise program is not only great for your heart, lungs and core stability; it tones, tightens and promotes weightloss while working every muscle group in your body.

With your dog by your side, happily partaking in all of your hard-work, **6 Legs to Fitness** will challenge your bodies and stimulate your minds while giving your dog a vital education.

6 Legs to Fitness not only builds muscles and healthy lifestyles, it builds a stronger bond and SYNERGY between you and your pooch!

SYNERGY
Activity Workbook

Brad Pattison

No Frills - No Gimmicks - No Masking
Just Pure Results!

SYNERGY DOG TRAINING

Hands-On Activity Book

The purpose of this workbook is to provide you with step by step guidance to successfully implement and track your training.

By no means do you want to unravel all your efforts, so giving your dog an edible treat at **any** time, is **forbidden**.

The following activities are based on teachings directly from Synergy and are followed by an area to track your activities with your dog.

It is best to refer back to the corresponding chapter in the book, if you need clarification about any of the exercises.

All the best & enjoy!

Brad

Chapter 1
Puppy Overview

Activity #1 Potty Training

When you first get a puppy or dog you need to show the new pet where to do their business. The most appropriate time to begin this type of training is first thing in the morning.

Step 1:

Put your pet on a six-foot leash and direct the dog to the designated area. This can be a dog run, an out-of-sight place in the yard or in a dog litter box. Speak calmly to your dog while walking to the designated spot. Your responsibility is to hold the leash and keep the dog in the area you have chosen. Allow the dog to sniff the ground and allow ample slack in the leash so the dog does not feel restricted while getting into position.

Step 2:

When the dog is sniffing the ground say to your dog "go pee pee" or say "go poo poo."

Step 3:

Wait until your dog begins to go pee, then address the dog and praise him/her with "good pee pee".

Step 4:

Pat your dog on the head and give a good strong praise with physical touch. Next the dog needs to finish up with the poo poo part. Allow the dog to re-position themselves to accommodate the next task.

Allow the dog to find the best spot in the designated area. Say, "Okay go poo poo" and say the dog's name.

Step 5:

When the dog has taken up the pooping position praise the dog quietly. Do not touch your dog at this time. When he/she is finished, praise in the same manner as with the pee experience.

Notes:

Activity #2 Potty Mishaps

Step 1:

Once you find the gift that your puppy has deposited, call your puppy. You will need to sit in the floor and talk to your puppy, ask if this was the right thing to do using a conversational tone. This conversation should last at least one minute.

Step 2:

Do not grab your puppy in a harsh way but do show your puppy the mistake. Hook your index finger between the collar and the neck do not allow your puppy to argue back.

If your puppy has attitude towards you and the situation then pin your puppy to the ground (Ch.7). Wait till the puppy has settled then continue speaking with conversational tone, making your puppy look at the mistake.

Step 3:

The next step is to carry on with your daily activity but do not have conversation with your puppy for fifteen minutes. No eye contact either. Another option is put your puppy outside.

Notes:

Notes:

Chapter 2
Toys & Play

Activity #1 Getting Creative

Write a list of safe toys that you could create for your dog. Remember not to have too many toys out all at once – the dog may begin to become confused about what is a toy and what is not.

Notes:

Notes:

Remember! Do not dump on your dog because you're being challenged. Your dog is depending on you. If you think you have it hard, place yourself in their shoes. Take a deep breath and take it one day at a time. Remember your dog doesn't sell you off and wipe their paws clean of you.

Chapter 3
Equipment

Activity #1 Leash and Collar

Please take the time to be sure that you are using the best equipment , not only for you, but especially for your dog.

You need a collar that reacts quickly, smoothly and of course, in a humane manner. A collar that does not release the tension from around the dog's neck is not the working mechanics you want for your dog.

Step 1:

Examine your leash. When looking at clasps, look for a stiff movement or a strong pinch so the clasp is securely closed.

Step 2:

Put your collar and leash on your dog and walk around with your dog for a bit. Notice how quickly it releases after you correct your dog. If it is not happening instantly – you need to replace your collar with something better – preferably a Martingale collar. You can purchase Hustle Up™ brand Martingale collars on my website at www.bradpattison.com

Step 3:

Put your dog in the umbilical position - leash around your waist, as you would a belt, but without using the belt loops. Take your dog for a walk. There should be about 2 - 2 ½ feet between you and your dog – enough to give them room, but enough that they are not within arm's reach. A 6 foot leash is your best length.

Notes:

Activity #2 Bedding

Step 1:

Forget about what you like or want or how it may look. Write down on a piece of paper the following considerations:

- Where will the dog be sleeping, indoors or outdoors?

- Is the dog coat short or long?

- How many seasons are there?

- What are the temperature ranges?

- What type of floor will be under the dog's bed, carpet, concrete, dirt, hard wood floor, linoleum or tile?

- Will the dog be sleeping under your bed, in a doghouse, on a wooden porch, grass or snow-covered surface?

Once you have answered the questions, you can make an informed decision about what to purchase for your dog based on their needs.

Notes:

Chapter 4
The Forbidden Zone

Activity #3 Couch

Step 1:

As the dog sets up to leap or climb onto the couch move a hand straight to the dog's face or chest. The face is your best option as it leads the dog to the right conclusion. Keep an open hand with palm out facing the dog. Meet the dog as the dog is in motion to get up on the couch.

Remember do not say anything verbally. The size of the dog will determine how much strength you will need to stop the dog. Imagine the dog running head first into a glass wall. This is what needs to be achieved.

Let's assume the dog successfully makes it on to the couch and will not get off. Grab on to the collar and pull the dog off the couch. When pulling the dog off the couch, your movement must be quicker than the dog's movement.

You should be pulling fast enough so the dog is scrambling to get to their feet. If this application is done too slow, the dog will continuously jump up on the couch. Dog wins, you lose!

Notes:

Notes:

Chapter 5
Hand Friendly

Activity # 1 Hand Friendly

Step 1:

Have you ever massaged your jaw or had somebody massage your jaw for you? Try it for the next three to five minutes.

Step 2:

Place your dog into a "down" position. Slowly move your hands across the body massaging slowly and gently. Once the eyes become heavy, stand above your dog's head and pull up slowly on their front legs gripping the paws.

Do this slowly. Now allow your dog's head to tilt back slightly. Massage out the front legs or as I call them, their arms.

Step 3:

Repeat the same procedure on the hind legs.

Notes:

Activity #2 Get to Know the Body

Step 1:

Spend the time touching their toes, taking their pulse. Feel how the ribs move similarly to ours. Find out where the stomach is and feel how much warmer it is than the spine.

Step 2:

Inspect your dog's paws, look at the nails and familiarize yourself with the shoulders. Move the limbs so you understand how they move. What are the limitations for stretching?

Step 3:

Check out the ears. Look to see if they need to be cleaned or better yet clean them just for fun (consult your local veterinarian first). Listen to your dog's breathing.

Memorize it because it may come in handy if you think that something is obstructing the airflow.

TIPS: Have fun. Move slowly & pay attention to your dog's needs.

Notes:

Chapter 6
Grooming

Activity #1 Care for the Coat

Step 1:

Brushing direction is from head to tip of tail.

Step 2:

Start in the middle of spine and brush to the under belly, do this on both sides of the dog.

Step 3:

Reverse brush direction starting at the hindquarters and brush the coat towards the head of the dog. Use short strokes.

Step 4:

Begin on the underbelly and brush upwards to the dog's spine, advancing around to the chest of the dog then brush the opposite side of the dog.

Notes:

Activity #2 Care for the Ears

How to Treat Ear Mites

Step1:

Moisten a tea bag with lukewarm water.

Step 2:

Dab inside the ear and let it sit for a couple of minutes. Roll the tea bag around inside the ear.

Step 3:

Repeat this twice a day. Complete the full cleaning practice for three days.

Step 4:

After three days, smell the ear. If you cannot smell anything then monitor, check and clean ears periodically. If there is still pungent odour after this treatment, take the dog to the veterinary clinic.

Notes:

Activity #3 Care for the Feet and Nails

Step 1:

When first approaching your dog, do a nail trimming massage to the dog's feet while the dog sleeps and speak quietly. Massage each foot slowly stretching the toes.

Step 2:

Start with the easiest nail and trim a small amount off of the nail 2 millimetres at a time.

Be careful not to clip too short. If you do, your dog will yelp and try and escape. Trust is a major factor. If you are kind and cause no harm you will be able to trim the nails without a fuss.

Step 3:

If a quick is cut there could be extensive bleeding. Apply a cool cloth around the dog's foot and have your dog stay settled in one spot in a down-stay. Keep your dog from getting up and walking away. The average time for bleeding to stop is twenty minutes. At local pet stores, you can find a stopper ointment for nails.

Notes:

Activity # 4 Care for the Teeth

Never use human toothpaste to brush your dog's teeth. Human toothpaste will make your dog very ill. Pet stores carry canine toothpaste and brushes.

Step 1:

Before you begin brushing your dog's teeth and gums, practice rubbing your index finger in your dog's mouth. Feel each individual tooth.

Step 2:

Massage the gums on both upper and lower jaws. This should be practiced a couple of times a day for four days before introducing the finger toothbrush.

Step 3:

After a day, follow up with toothpaste on the finger toothbrush.

Visually get to know the dog's mouth, color of teeth, gums, and tongue. Does your dog's breath smell all the time or once in a while?

Notes:

Chapter 7
Establishing Alpha

Activity #1 Umbilical Training - Puppies

Step 1:

Take your six-foot leash and place it around your waist, as you would a belt. Do not use the belt loops. Hold the handle of the leash in your left hand and hold the clasp in your right. Slip the clasp through the handle or loop. Feed it through until the leash becomes taut around your waist. Fasten the clasp to the MARTINGALE collar.

Step 2:

This is hands-free training. You will not touch the leash with your hands. Begin walking around, turn sharply and step in front of your dog. Now change direction moving quickly.

Two hours of umbilical training daily is the minimum requirement. The two hours can be broken up into smaller sessions, if your schedule requires it. Watching television or sitting down for an hour or more with the dog attached to your waist is also classified as training.

Keep in mind while working with the umbilical exercises, the bottom line is that you are controlling the dog's movement. You make all choices as to when to move and how far you are going.

You are the boss and you always win! When you are challenged and the dog wants to pull to the side or backwards, then it is your responsibility to continue to move forward until the dog gives in. At this point, you may choose to end training for the day.

Notes:

Activity #2 Umbilical Training – Adult Dogs

This section applies to an adult dog, where there may be habits to break. Therefore, the learning process is structured differently

Watch for the following corrections during umbilical training

Step 1:

Once your dog is in umbilical, got o the front door and open it but do not go out. Did the dog try and walk out the front door?

Step 2:

Continue walking around and notice if you are holding on to the leash? During umbilical you should never hold the leash.

Step 3:

Did you verbally guide your dog?

Ask a friend or family member to log how many times you ask your dog do to something. Keep track of how many times you repeat the same request and how quickly you repeat yourself after the first time.

At the end of the day look at your list and you will see a pattern showing you how many times you make the same request.

Step 4:

Did you repeat yourself?

Test yourself. Take your dog outside and ask your dog to sit without using a leash to provoke the action. Next, ask your dog to lay down, again without using the leash.

Now for fun, let your dog off the leash and call your dog in ninety seconds. If your dog responded immediately then you have taught your dog well, so far. If your dog did not respond immediately or at all, your dog certainly has not made the error. You need to continue practicing.

Notes:

Activity #3 Non-Verbal Training

Step 1:

The main focus behind this is obvious – be quiet.

Practice umbilical training, inside or outside, without any verbal communication.

Track you activity with your dog, noticing what you find easy and/or difficult about the exercise and how your dog responds.

Notes:

Activity #4 How to Train Hands Free

Step 1:

After attaching the leash around your waist, attach the leash to the dog's Martingale collar. Your dog may get excited, assuming it will be going for a walk outside. Ignore this behaviour and begin walking around the house with your dog watching you and following.

Step 2:

As you turn a corner in the house, do not touch the lead with your hand. Ignore the leash. Go into the kitchen and grab two cans of food out of the cupboard. The reason I want you to hold onto the cans, one in either hand is to keep your hands occupied.

This will help you break the habit of touching the leash. As the next few days pass and you continue this exercise, you will graduate to talking on the phone and drinking a glass of water as you walk around.

Step 3:

Grab the garbage, take it outside begin moving large objects around, all the while having your dog attached to you. Here is an important point to keep in mind. Pulling is not allowed at any time. If this happens drop one hand down on the tight leash and give it a sharp correction.

Notes:

Activity #5 How to Pin Your Dog

I recommend you do a minimum of twenty repetitions to a maximum of thirty. Reactions to be aware of when applying this exercise, are grumbling, whining, heavy breathing, yipping, shrieking, clawing, thrashing and kicking back the head.

What your dog has been able to get away with in the past will be one factor as to how your dog responds to this exercise. While working with your dog during this exercise do not speak to your dog. If the dog tries to escape and whimpers or screams, hold on tight to the collar.

Do not let go. When the dog settles down, continue the exercise. With many dogs I have found a consistency with the dogs acting up and fighting back. This behaviour usually begins between the seventh and ninth repetition.

If your dog snaps or bites ,muzzle the dog with a properly fitted muzzle.

Step 1:

Size the collar (martingale) so you have one thumb width between the two loops when pulled snug. Pull snug from the top of the neck below the ears. Size correctly if the collar is tight or too loose. Remove the leash if it is fastened to the Martingale collar.

Step 2:

Ask the dog to come with you as you guide the dog to an open space on the floor. Gently holding onto the Martingale collar, guide the dog to a non-slippery floor surface. Carpet, Astroturf and rubber floor are good training surfaces. Good outdoor training surfaces would be grass or pavement.

Step 3:

Sit down on the floor with your legs spread open in the letter V. Position the dog facing you between your legs.

Step 4:

The dog should be in a sit position looking at you about twelve inches from your chest. Place your right thumb and left thumb under the dog's jawbone. Move your thumbs towards the dog until the thumbs are between the martingale collar and the dog's throat.

This is very important to have your thumbs in this position. Apply pressure downward on the Martingale Collar until it becomes taut against the back of the dog's neck. Stop, take a look to see and feel that the dog has no obstruction to the throat.

Step 5:

Apply pressure in a down direction. Apply 3% more strength than the dog is applying. Do not jerk downward suddenly; instead, apply steady pressure.

Keep your elbows bent; use only the amount of strength suggested. Hold this position until the dog begins to lie down. Apply the 3% until you have moved the dog into a down position.

Once the dog is down, relax for a moment (five seconds). While applying this procedure, keep in mind that you want the dog to give in - this is not forced training with any type of jerking motion.

Step 6:

You have accomplished the first half of a repetition now let's finish a full rep. Hold the Martingale collar in the same place, as you move your hands up and underneath the dog's jaw you will need to stabilize the jaw so it is firmly sitting in your hands on the meaty part of the thumb. Once your hands are in position, lift the dog up and place in a sit position.

When placing your dog into the "sit", over exaggerate the whole sit movement by moving your dog past the "sit". This will require you to take the dog into an upright position so the two front paws float off the ground by one inch. Do not lift the front paws off the ground more than this (two inches).

Notes:

Activity #6 Your Child as Alpha

Your child can practice the same exercises with your dog that you do, but please keep the following in mind:

- You are the Alpha. If a situation takes place and a family member cannot control the situation and win, then you must step in and assist the person in need of your help.

- Everyone backs up the handler who is handling the dog at the time.

- Where do I fit in? This is directed at the pup or dog. Body language, consistency and perseverance are needed to help the dog learn. The dog will have no other choice because you have not granted them any options.

- Your child will always finish any type of training done for any given amount of time in a win position. With your help and guidance, this will be accomplished. "Win" is as important as teaching a "Stay".

- You, as the parent, will need to correct the dog if any pulling takes place. The child usually is not quick enough or strong enough to handle the beginning stages of discipline.

- The child will always enter and exit any doorway first, with the puppy following. The child eats before puppy and the child pushes the puppy off after playing on the floor if the puppy is on top. The puppy is never allowed on or in the child's bed. This also includes the couch.

- Teach your child not to scream when the puppy chases them, as this encourages a dominant position for the puppy.

Notes:

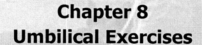

Chapter 8
Umbilical Exercises

Activity # 1 Educating Your Dog to Watch You

Step 1:

Stand up, put the leash around your waist, slide the clasp through the handle loop, snug it up around your waist and hook up to your dog's collar.

Walk into your kitchen, pretend you have to answer the phone, walk to the front door and stop with the door wide open.

Step 2:

Go sit down, and grab a pencil.

Write your answers after each of the following questions:

Who was leading? _____

Was the leash tight at all? _____

When you turned to answer the phone, did you step on your dog's paw?

_____

Did the dog try and walk out the front door? _____

Did you hold onto the leash? _____

Did you verbally guide your dog? _____

Did you repeat yourself? _____

Did you walk slower than normal? _____

When you stopped at any point was the leash relaxed without you making adjustments to the dogs positioning by shuffling closer to the dog?

_____

Notes:

** Go back to Chapter 7 to get more guidance in successful umbilical training if needed.

Activity #2 Educating For Stairs

Step 1:

Teaching a dog to stay out from under your feet can be fun. Implement a game of stepping lightly on the dog's feet. Get the dog to become aware your feet are capable of tagging or stepping on their paws. This type of training exercise should be done in fun, with a moderate tone of seriousness.

Notes:

Activity #3 Educating For Doors & Doorways

Step1:

Stand at a doorway and when the dog proceeds to exit ahead of you close the door on the dog. Be careful and do not be a brute.

When closing the door, begin door movement as the dog is encroaching in the doorway space. Bonk the dog with the door enough to stir the dog's thoughts. Now the dog will be aware.

Step 2:

You exit, enter and pass through all doorways first, with the dog following. If the dog bolts or tries to lead you, make an abrupt turn and step off quickly going in the opposite direction from the door you were about to walk through.

Make your dog sit at all doorways for a minimum of five seconds. We do not want your dog to rush to its death.

Notes:

Chapter 9
On-Lead Basics

Activity # 1 Teaching "Sit"

Step 1:

Put the lead around your waist in the umbilical position; and attach the clasp of the lead to the floating ring on the Martingale collar.

Begin walking around with your hands not touching the leash. Stop and grab the lead eight to ten inches above the clasp attached to the collar.

Step 2:

Pull straight up holding tight to the lead. Pull the lead up until the collar begins to tighten and the dog begins to sit.

If the dog does not begin to sit, pull the lead up until the collar is tight and the dog will make a choice to sit. If your dog does not sit and begins to flail, pull up on the lead until the front paws float off the ground by about a two-inch clearance.

Wait until your dog begins to move into the "sit" position, and then relax the lead. Continue moving around and stop.

Repeat this exercise until the dog sits on its own as soon as you stop. This is when you can stop working this exercise during this training period.

Once your dog is sitting seventy percent of the time when you come to a stop, you can progress to the next step.

Step 3:

Remove the lead from your waist; leave the lead attached to the dog. Hold the lead in one hand, turn around and face your dog. Walk backwards with the dog following you.

Stop and stand in front of your dog with perfect posture, standing straight up. Place feet shoulder width apart. Look at your dog and wait for your dog to sit. No verbal chit chat.

Once your dog sits again, back up ten feet with the leash attached to the collar. Stop and stand directly in front of your dog keeping a space of ten feet in distance. Your dog should not move around.

If your dog turns their head away, move directly in front of your dog. Keep your position until your dog sits.

Continue this exercise until your dog sits immediately when you turn and face your dog. Praising your dog is the step to follow once you get consistent results.

Only when your dog sits immediately are you encouraged to praise your dog with kind loving petting and patting to the head and body.

Notes:

Activity #2 Teaching "Stay"

Step 1:

Place your dog in a "sit "or "down", keyword "place". What I mean by this is, physically move your dog to an area and place the dog into a sit or down position. Use no verbal commands with this exercise. Be patient. You will see success unfold as long as you stay calm and firm.

Step 2:

Physically move your dog to a new spot or location. Next, stand in front of your dog. Do not speak. Now allow ten seconds to pass. Praise the dog with a simple pat on the head.

Step 3:

Have the dog move with you to a new spot. Place the dog in a sit or down. Square off in front of the dog and say nothing. Count twenty seconds. Repeat the praise and a new position.

Gradually increase the time your dog is in a stay. Once you hit the three-minute point, our next goal is five minutes.

When time is up, place the dog back in the "stay" position and say nothing. If the dog breaks again, repeat by placing your dog in a "stay". Repeat this until you have your dog stay for the required period of time you selected.

Step 4:

Once your dog can stay for three minutes as you stand in front of them, you can move on to the next step. You will repeat the beginning stages by placing your dog in a "stay". This time I want you to step backwards until you are approximately five feet away and wait thirty seconds. Step back another five feet and wait for thirty seconds.

When one minute has passed, walk back to the dog and praise them by patting on the head.

Step 5:

Repeat the same exercise ten times at various time intervals between ten seconds and sixty seconds. When you have ten successful stays at ten feet, you can begin to increase the distance, working your way up to fifty feet in five-foot increments.

This is all non-verbal training to get your dog to "stay". When your dog breaks from the designated stay spot, you must place the dog in the exact spot and begin again.

To get your dog to come to you crouch down and open your arms. Verbally and physically praise your dog when they come to you.

Notes:

Activity #3 Teaching "Stop"

"Stop, start" is the exercise but the focal point is definitely on the word. "STOP." To begin, start strong and end strong.

Step 1:

Step one places your dog in a "sit-stay". Stand in front of your dog at a distance of two feet between the two of you. Slowly increase the distance to four feet.

Step 2:

Call your dog to come forward, as soon as your dog begins movement forward, firmly and loud say, "STOP."

As you say "stop", move your hand directly forward at head height of the dog until your hand meets the dog's movement. It's sort of like you banging your head on a low ceiling or cupboard. But this time, your hands are acting as the ceiling and the dog runs into your hands.

This exercise needs firm quick movement. Keep in mind when you move forward towards the dog, your body language is confirming and reinforcing the command "STOP"!

Notes:

Activity #4 Teaching "Come"

If the dog does not respond to you immediately the dog has all off-lead rights revoked and is placed back on-lead. "No ifs, ands, or buts!"

Step 1:

Allow the dog to be free for five seconds, call your dog back, remember to crouch down and praise heavily for coming to you.

Step 2:

Set your dog free and call them back after fifteen seconds, continuing this exercise for a few minutes. Allow the dog to have time to do dog things. Return to the exercise and have fun.

Notes:

Activity #5 Teaching "Heel"

Step1:

Attach the lead in the umbilical fashion.

Begin walking and taking your dog around and in and out of obstacles, such as trees, poles, parking meters and anything else you encounter.

Step 2:

Once your dog is paying attention to you and the dog is walking with you, praise and say "good heel". Whenever your dog heels with you at the corner, on the street, in the park or in the house, confirm verbally what the dog has accomplished in a positive manner. Implement the phrase "Good heel."

Notes:

Here is an advanced step for the dog enthusiast who is doing great with the previous exercises. This is where your dog and is off-lead.

Step 3:

The moment your dog catches up to you and walks with you, acknowledging your position, then pet the dog on the head and say "good heel." We want to work heel in as a positive. The dog wants to be with you or better yet, the dog has no problem slowing down or speeding up to walk beside you.

Notes:

Activity #6 Teaching "Down"

Step1:

Sit in front of your dog on some grass or carpet. Attach the leash. Hold it for a safety measure if doing this exercise outside.

Step 2:

With no verbal communication, I want you to place your dog in a "sit". Once the dog is in a sit, motion a hand in front of the dog's face and draw the hand downward to the ground.

Step 3:

The hand that is doing nothing can hold onto the leash and draw the lead downward applying pressure smoothly. If the dog fights or flails, restrict movement by pulling steadily downward with more pressure.

Step 4:

Once the dog is down, sit the dog up and begin again. As the dog clues into the exercise you should be applying less effort with the hand that is guiding the lead.

As soon as your dog lies down without any guidance, praise your dog verbally saying the word "down". "Good down Tina, good down". Now begin again or take a break from the exercise and come back to it.

Remember finish on a strong positive. That means lots of verbal praise with lots of pats. This exercise can be quite time consuming, with many repetitions and you may see no results in the training for a few days. Persist, be consistent, be diligent and do not become lazy.

Notes:

Chapter 10
Patience Training

Activity #1 - 3, 5, 10 minute "Sit-Stay"

Step 1:

Place your dog in a "stay" beside a tree in the park and ask your dog to stay. Walk away.

Step 2:

Time your dog to stay for three minutes, this may not happen right away so begin your dog at twenty seconds.

Praise your dog for staying and repeat the process, this time for thirty seconds.

When we do this exercise at the beginning we never have the dog come running to us after they have accomplished the allotted time.

Keep your dog in the "stay" position and you go back to your dog. This helps to ensure the dog doesn't flee. With you returning, it teaches the dog you will be coming back.

Your responsibility is eventually to make distance between you and your dog as far as possible and out of the dog's line of vision. If the dog breaks you need to catch your dog without saying a word. Return the dog to the original position. Show your hand for "stay" and/or say the word "stay" or "wait." Do not turn your back to the dog. Walk backwards and stay square to the dog. Turning your back shows weakness.

Step 3:

Once you have achieved a three minute stay, increase this time to five minutes, gradually building it to ten minutes.

The time to practice this is after some playtime has been granted or after exercise. When the dog has learned about patience, test the dog immediately when you get to the park before any play has been granted.

Stop at a café for a drink and leave your dog in a 'wait" position tied up and monitor for any whining or other verbal communication. If your dog is behaving properly praise him after a few minutes.

Watch for chewing on the lead or shivering and anxiety, or any behaviour that is not normal for your dog.

Monitor any defensive behaviour and use your voice to interrupt your dog as you approach, not when you get to the dog. Jumping up is not tolerated and needs to be corrected immediately. Tie the lead shorter if you need t, so your dog can't jump.

Notes:

Chapter 11
Off-Lead Basics

Activity #1 Teaching Off-Lead "Sit"

Step 1:

Begin walking with your dog. Now stop and turn to face your dog. The dog sits and you emphasize the word "sit".

Step 2:

When the dog does not sit immediately place a hand on the dog's head and stroke the hand to the rear of the dog, applying slightly more pressure, as you get closer to the hindquarters.

Step 3:

Begin again and repeat the steps. If the dog sits immediately when you turn and face the dog. Great!

Step 4:

This time start walking for thirty feet. Stop. Stay exactly where you stopped. Do not face your dog. Praise the dog if the dog goes into an automatic sit. If the dog did not sit then stroke the spine moving from the head to the hindquarters.

Repeat until you have consistent, automatic sit without touching the dog.

Notes:

Activity # 2 Teaching Off-Lead "Stay"

Step1:

Put the collar and leash on and let's go to the front door. Okay, lay your dog down in the open doorway.

Step 2:

Attach the leash to the doorknob on the inside of the door and tell your dog to "wait" or "stay".

Step 3:

Leave your dog at the entrance. Watch from a distance that the dog is not moving about.

Step 4:

If the dog did not move for thirty seconds, praise the dog.

Repeat the stay or wait and exit the room. Leave for one minute and praise.

Step 5:

This time try going outside. Stand outside for a couple of minutes. If the dog gets up and tries to walk away from the down, the door will shut and the dog will be restricted by the leash.

Step 6:

Place your dog (using the non-verbal method) in the "down-stay" position. Walk away again to the same spot you were standing outside. Wait up to two minutes and praise your dog if the dog did not break.

At any given time, if the dog breaks and does not stay settled in the stay, you are required to place the dog back in that same position. Once you are consistent with the dog staying, then release the lead and begin the process again, always keeping an eye on your dog.

This is a lengthy process possibly requiring weeks of work. But you will have a great dog in the long run.

Notes:

Activity #3 Teaching Off-Lead "Heel"

Step 1:

Go for a walk with the dog on-lead. When the dog is heeling with you drop the leash, then stop and have the dog sit.

Step 2:

Begin moving forward with the dog walking beside you.

Step 3:

When the dog starts to get in front of you step on the dragging leash. It's a quickstep on and release the leash.

Continue walking and every time the dog begins to lead you step on the leash. Eventually, she will stay close to you in the correct heel position.

Step 4:

Next, when you are walking with the dog, turn around and go in the opposite direction. The dog will follow and catch up to you.

Be quick when you are working this exercise. If you move slowly you will lose the dog's interest and the training will lose its value.

Notes:

Turn in a circle with the dog watching you and keeping in the "heel" position. One game to play is tapping the dog's toes with your foot lightly and play tag. With this game have the dog on umbilical.

Activity #4 Teaching Off-Lead "Come"

Step 1:

Place your dog in a "stay" for one minute, back up twenty steps, say "hustle" then turn and start running.

Step 2:

Yell out the dog's name as you begin running. When the dog catches up to you and passes you, quickly turn around and go in the opposite direction.

Your dog will turn and catch up to you again.

Step 3:

Once again turn and the dog will need to catch you. When the dog catches you, really praise the dog!

Repeat this exercise starting at five feet distance and increasing your distance by five feet, only when the dog has done it three times perfectly. Do not rush in expanding the distance.

Take your time, work towards a win/win. Never leave training on a negative, always a positive and give your dog lots of loving.

Notes:

Activity #5 Off-Lead Road Crossing

This exercise requires both training and trust in yourself and the dog in which you have invested so many hours of training. Why I am stressing this so much?

Factor in everything and anything that you can imagine that could go wrong and remember that they are real possibilities. You're responsible for your dog's safety as well as your own when implementing these lessons in the off-lead chapters.

Responsibility and ownership is strictly on your shoulders and your dog trusts you!

Step 1:

Off-lead road crossing is serious and well rewarded every time you and your dog cross the road without a leash. Your dog is expected to know the command "STOP" without creeping or inching forward. The stop has to be definite and exact.

Approach a corner with your dog on lead and make sure the dog's attention is on you and only you. No flaky daydreaming allowed.

Step 2:

Stop briefly, eight feet from the curb on the sidewalk to confirm you have your dog's undivided attention.

Step 3:

Cross the road with lead in hand and settle your dog on the adjacent sidewalk.

Step 4:

This time, cross again but allow the dog to cross with the lead still attached to the collar and dragging along the ground.

Practice this a half dozen times. Cross quickly, slowing the walking pace down, reversing direction continuously challenging your dog to be alert and watch you with its full attention.

While I encourage you to give lots of positive praise, also I caution you not to over excite your dog and lose the frame of mind you have been working towards.

Undivided attention is crucial for the next step.

Step 5:

Remove the leash completely. Practice this in a low traffic area with ample visual access, so you can monitor the traffic.

Ensure you have ample time to slow down the on-coming traffic, if need be. For example, if your dog decides not to listen to you, strays away from the sidewalk or decides to do something else, you then have sufficient time to ensure your dog stays safe.

Think ahead. Work with your dog in close quarters at the beginning and slowly expand the distance between you and the dog. This can help ensure safe training.

Use verbal commands such as "let's go", "okay", "come" and apply the various hand signals you have learned to assist your dog.

Notes:

Activity #6 Off-Lead Stop up to 150 Ft

Your hand signal is to show one or two arms straight above your shoulder beside your head. Big body movement helps your dog see the signal at a long distance, or when the light is low, at dusk or dawn. Show both arms and hands like you're demonstrating a touchdown in American football.

Whistling is a great sound signal, as well as clapping or a crisp verbal word. Whistles or other sound devises are great, but not practical in all situations.

Step 1:

Begin working at a ten-foot distance with your dog and give a five-minute "sit" or "down-stay". Call forward, decrease the time your dog waits to be called and increase the distance. End training on an up-beat note, with positive outcomes.

Work up to When your dog stays & you get seventy five-feet away, leave your dog there for ten minutes. Start fluctuating the time from five minutes to eight minutes then up to ten minutes. Depending on how much time you are spending on training.

Monitor your dog for boredom or fatigue. Quit training if either one is affecting your dog. We want to develop your dog, not fail her. Finish off with a twenty second "down-stay", then praise her to "go play".

To break the one hundred foot barrier, do the exact same training as you do with the seventy-five foot exercise.

Notes:

Chapter 12
Five SUPER COOL Commands for your Dog

Activity #1 How to Teach "Rug"

Do not begin teaching this exercise or any of the other exercises when you need to have your request met. Teach this and educate before the need arises. We will consider this preparation for up and coming situations.

Step 1:

Grab your dog and place them on a lead.

Step 2:

Walk your dog to the rug by the door you come in and place your dog on that one spot. This is the spot the dog will go directly to upon entering. This spot should not be more than five feet from the doorway.

Step 3:

Tell the dog "stay on the rug".

Leave them there until you are ready for the dog to move.

Notes:

Activity #2 How to Teach "Bed"

When introducing the bed to the dog, I always advise clients to take the dog out during the day and exercise the dog well. Well enough so when play and exercise time is over, the dog will want to have a nap.

Step 1:

As you retire her for a nap, tell the dog when the dog gets onto the bed, "Okay go to bed", "Good dog this is your BED"

"Have a sleep in your new BED". Emphasize the key word bed.

Step 2:

What I would like you to do when you verbally tell the dog to go to bed is allow the dog to get to the bed before you do. When the dog steps onto the bed praise the dog "Good boy/girl, that's your bed, now stay there."

Step 3:

When the dog wakes up, praise them for sleeping on the bed with pats to the body and speaking in a gentle tone.

During the first week, introduce the dog to the bed by leaving the dog to rest on the bed in a "stay". When time for bed, introduce the bed again to the dog. Express the word "Bed" as your keyword.

Have fun with this command. Practice periodically during the middle of the day and in the early evening for about a month. The dog will associate the word BED and seek refuge to lie down.

Notes:

Activity # 3 How to Teach "Truck or Car"

Show the dog the place you want them to go to, do this twice. It may be the boat tied up to the dock or it may be the back of the truck. Regardless of the vehicle, your dog can succeed at understanding the request if shown and encouraged.

Step 1:

First begin with walking your dog to the car, tell your dog "let's go to the car".

Step 2:

Now walk six feet away and ask your dog to go to the car, leave a door open so the dog has an end point. Now if the dog does not go to the car, walk your dog towards the car.

Step 3:

Allow the dog to enter the car when you are a couple of feet away from the open door. When the dog jumps in the car, get crazy with praise! Now try again from ten feet away.

Step 4:

Keep trying at the eight to ten foot mark. When the dog does it and accomplishes the request, expand the distance to fifteen feet then twenty, twenty five, and so on.

Notes:

Activity #4 How to Teach "Back"

Step 1:

Stand at the front door or gate, say "back" then open up the door quickly, causing the dog to move back. Do this exercise for four days or until the dog moves back upon the door being open.

You will notice a dog will learn the door can only go so far so the dog will only move back the required distance. Once your dog has learned about the door or gate proceed onto the next step.

Step 2:

When you say the word "BACK", turn and face your dog. Move the dog backwards by walking straight into it. If you step on the paws, the dog will clear out of your way quicker and acknowledge your command.

Practice this numerous times.

Notes:

Activity #5 How to Teach "Who's There?"

When you hear a strange sound, "Who's there?" is a great command to teach a dog to bark, growl, pace or become alert. This is a great way to get your dog to appear like the dog will protect you. Depending upon the personality of your dog this is a good command to practice for safety.

Step 1:

Whenever you hear or see something strange, react in a concerned manner and get your dog involved. Never allow your dog to disappear from your sight and always practice this with the dog on-lead or in a confined area such as your home or the inside of a vehicle. This is one way to warn someone to stay away.

Notes:

Notes:

Chapter 14
Corrections

Activity #1 Under Jaw

What I would like you to remember about this correction is, forty-five degrees. Forty-five degrees is the angle your hand travels upward to strike the dog underneath the jaw.

The jaw is made of bone so you need to know - do not strike upward at a ninety-degree angle.

Your hand needs to be tight, clenched and firm. A soft hand makes for a pointless correction.

Finally, when correcting under the jaw, you need to move your hand very quickly. If the dog decides to move you will miss and the dog will get the last laugh.

Ha Ha.

Notes:

Activity #2 Across Snout

Correcting across the face follows the same forty-five degree angle rule that I mentioned earlier. The beginning point for the strike zone is the middle of the head between the ears and the eyes. Never strike downward onto the head, eyes or nose. The nose is made from cartilage and is fragile. I like people to understand this type of correction, so turn to a friend or spouse, take your hand and slide it down their face and then run because your friend or spouse won't like it.

Notes:

Activity #3 The Hand Drop

The hand drop is a fake.

You fake out your dog pretending you are going to drop your hand across the face but you don't. A hand drop is always a fake and it is for you to use to get the attention of your dog, clean and simple.

You would do this anytime your dog is trying to lead or pull you when on a leash.

Notes:

Activity #4 Jail

Any time when your dog creates a volatile situation or challenges your position, you need to act immediately.

Control and isolate your dog with your hands. Act quickly and use a verbal tone and body language that clearly states, you will not tolerate such behaviour.

Place your dog in JAIL and do it quickly! Thirty seconds tops and then you need to vanish from the dog's sight.

When placing a dog in jail they are left in a sitting position. The leash is at a length that if they choose to lay down their collar becomes uncomfortable.

When a dog needs to sit and settle and their behaviour is being controlled, they find out quite quickly that jail is not their choice.

Jail time can last from fifteen minutes up to forty-five minutes, depending upon the "crime".

When releasing your dog from jail it is not a time for pats on the head or rear. When releasing your dog, keep in mind that if you speak in an excited tone then the dog will feel it is being praised for hanging out in jail.

Instead, speak firmly and do not allow your dog to go outside immediately. Take at least twenty minutes to warm up to your dog after the release from jail.

Notes:

Activity #5 Time Out

Poles, trees, benches, railing or any object that is fastened down will work for time out. Be creative when placing your dog in time out.

Time out can be beside you or fifty feet away. People are allowed to say hi to your dog as long as your dog respects the visitor.

Speaking with your dog is encouraged, keep in mind you are using a medium tone. The amount of time to be spent in time out is up to you.

You can test your dog to find out if the changed behaviour is legitimate. If you are convinced your dog has acknowledged the situation and improved on it, by all means carry on and enjoy your time together.

Notes:

Notes:

Chapter 14
The Big "No-No"s

Activity #1 No Barking

Stopping through Interruption

Step 1:

We always want to interrupt the mistake so the dog never makes a complete error. When a puppy gets geared up to bark it is accompanied by a change in attitude. So what you need to do is say "BOO" fast, loud, and in a hi pitch.

That will interrupt the puppy from building up the overzealous attitude. This needs to be said, as the growl from the puppy gets deeper in tone or if the tone is coming from the belly.

If the puppy barks, correcting under the jaw is required. Refer back to Chapter 14. The correction needs to be firm and quick without any hesitation.

Notes:

Activity #2 No Barking
Dealing with Separation Anxiety

Step 1:

Trick your dog into believing you have left the home

Step 2:

Wait quietly on the other side of the door with the door unlocked so you can burst back into the house with a loud "HEY, WHAT ARE YOU DOING BARKING?...NO NOISE." Followed up with correcting the dog under the jaw and placing the dog in a "sit".

Step 3:

Depart from the house again, repeating as often as possible. Homework for this exercise is for you to lengthen the period of time you leave the dog alone. This can be accomplished at the park, outside a café and of course, at home.

Step 4:

Every time you leave your dog lengthen the time by a minute or two each time. Come back often, praise your dog for not barking and strive for 100% results.

Step 5:

If your dog has not made any noise for fifteen minutes and he/she usually barks at that time, go back and praise your dog for not making a sound.

Step 6:

Leave the dog again, this time try and go for seventeen minutes, praise again if your dog did not make a sound. Oops, the dog barked once at the sixteen-minute mark.

Step 7:

As soon as the dog makes that first sound you need to appear immediately. Walk with your shoulders square to the dog and move with purpose.

This body language will help you to educate your dog that the bark was not acceptable. Speak in a low, deep voice and say "NO NOISE."

You will need to practice this exercise every time the dog makes noise when it should not.

Notes:

:tivity #3 No Jumping Up

Step 1:

When the dog is in front of you I want you watch him as he begins to jump up.

Step 2:

Quickly place your hand in front of the dog's head, moving your hand in a downward direction meeting the dog's head as it tries to jump up.

Keep your hand firm so when the dog collides with your hand he/she feels it and takes special notice in the discomfort they caused themselves.

Step 3:

Follow this hand action with a verbal command "OFF, STAY OFF!" If you have successfully accomplished this, then you will need to follow up with a simple show of the hand in front of the dog's face when he/she approaches and is about to jump. You can follow up this hand gesture with a firm "No."

Notes:

Activity # 4 No Digging

Step 1:

When you see him pawing at the dirt, interrupt the behaviour with a firm, deep loud, "NO, leave it!"

Step 2:

When the dog moves away from the area in question give him a toy to distract him.

Monitor him for further digging actions.

Brad's Tips:

Always address the issue of the destroyed property immediately. Use a firm low verbal tone " No digging". Physically show the dog the destruction. Place in jail for a minimum twenty minutes. Do not speak to the criminal. Let the criminal out of jail. Say nothing for a minimum of ten minutes.

Notes:

Notes:

Chapter 15
Speaking to Your Dog

Activity #1 Tone of Voice

Here are your verbal words to practice.

Practice these three tones:

      1) high pitch happy, medium tone,

      2) normal voice

      3) stern, deep tone .

        Sit – Stay - Stop – Come – Wait – Hustle Up - Who's There?

Notes:

Activity #2 Pronouncing Syllables & Consonants

Clarity when pronouncing these words or the words you come up with to train your dog to respond to is important. Mumbling a command in a life and death situation is not going to bring your dog to an abrupt stop if needed.

Step 1:

Please study and practice saying each of these words or your own set of words with clarity.

Come, Stay, Okay, Wait, Let's go, Sit, Stop, Down, Lay down, No noise, Hustle up, Go to bed, Who's there? Go see Mom, go see Dad, Go to the truck.

Notes:

Review of the All-Important Basics:

Activity #1 Basic Commands

Basic commands in the park are essential to ensure your dog's safety and the safety of other dogs and/or people in the park or out on the street.

Basic commands to practice are: come, sit, stay, relax, hustle, heel, and now.

"Come": use it to get your dog to catch up to you quickly.

"Sit": stop your dog and get the dog's undivided attention. No movement is allowed until you say so.

"Stay": is clearly stating that the dog is to do nothing but stay focused on you and your next request. The dog is not allowed to venture off and socialize. Even if another dog comes to say "hello", your dog does not move.

"Relax": this is a great word to educate your dog with. This is a word used when animosity is building between two or more dogs and you want your dog to submit and not be the aggressor. When using this word you are now expected to be the enforcer and aggressor if a situation breaks out.

"Hustle": Your dog responds to this word and drops what they are doing and immediately pursues you.

"Heel": Simple and straight forward, your dog takes up a side position either on your right or left, acknowledging you with eye contact.

"Now": This word is used in situations when the dog is being lackadaisical in their movement, either to sit, lay down, come, leave it or any other request, including listening, you have asked. Use this command with a very firm, strong and deep tone.

Notes: